Saint-Émilion

TEXT BY
BÉATRICE MASSENET
EMMANUELLE PONSAN-DANTIN
FRANÇOIS QUERRE

PHOTOGRAPHS BY
GUILLAUME DE LAUBIER

Saint-Émilion

The Châteaux, Winemakers, and Landscapes
of Bordeaux's Famed Region

ABRAMS

NEW YORK

CONTENTS

47
FIRST GREAT
CLASSIFIED GROWTHS

113
GREAT CLASSIFIED
GROWTHS

FOREWORD

BY SERENA SUTCLIFFE, DIRECTOR OF SOTHEBY'S INTERNATIONAL WINE DEPARTMENT

The spirit of Saint-Émilion's wines is inextricably linked to the spirit of the place. One comes in glorious liquid form, the other in the character of the people, the châteaux and the landscape. Saint-Émilion is the absolute example of history in the glass, blending the vine, the wine and the way of life into a cohesive entity. However, I am sure the Saint-Émilionnais see each day more practically, as do all those who earn their living on and from the land, and this book lets you into their homes in a very direct way.

Châteaux are not often described as "homes", but Saint-Émilion is somewhat exceptional among Bordeaux's finest wines because so many wine properties are lived in by the families who own them and make the wine. The region must be the most "organic" of all the grand names in the wine world, where almost everyone is in some way touched by the vine. Saint-Émilion is where neighbours think and breathe the same local, life-enhancing end product, rivalries are also friendships and acquiring experience and knowledge is a shared aim.

There is, at the same time, huge diversity in Saint-Émilion, in its micro-regions and soil types, in its architecture and in the grandeur, or modesty, of its wine estates. Seigneurial properties sit beside comfortable, small manor houses; relatively large vineyard holdings rub shoulders with tiny, jewel-like plots. Families that have centuries-old roots in their land have been joined by outsiders from France and further afield who answered the call, and the lure, of Saint-Émilion. A noticeable feature of these newcomers is that they never seem grafted on to the region and the community, but are quickly absorbed into Saint-Émilion's welcoming web of warmth. Maybe this is a reflection of the generosity of the wines, which come out to greet you on every occasion, whether they are young or old, regardless of their place in the hierarchy.

Drinking Saint-Émilion is, indeed, like coming home.

THE JURADE
OF SAINT-ÉMILION:
A TIME-HONOURED TRADITION

In 1152, when Duchess Eleanor of Aquitaine acceded to the throne of England through her marriage with Henry Plantagenet (later Henry II), she entrusted her son Richard the Lionheart with several missions. Though he started off by reorganizing the city of London, creating the office of First Lord Mayor, the small town of Saint-Émilion, in the French part of his kingdom, was also among his concerns. He granted to the jurats, the town notables, special powers and rights. After Richard was killed in Chalus, in 1199, his brother John Lackland, king of England, summoned the wealthy notables of Saint-Émilion to his Falaise castle, in Normandy, and presented them with a charter establishing the creation of the Jurade with the assigned task of ruling the town and nearby villages.

Before that, after the year 800, eight parishes of the city had gathered around the figure of the hermit Émilion. A few centuries later, the whole little region was under the rule of the Saint-Émilion jurats for all civil and military matters. Among the many activities practised by the citizens and peasants in the region, winemaking — from vines planted in ancient Roman times — became increasingly important through the centuries thanks to the reinforcement of security on roads. The Jurade, made up of well-off citizens and winemakers of Saint-Émilion, set up a firm and vigilant legislation, setting high standards and avoiding easy solutions. Thus the great wines of Saint-Émilion were born, and so was their indisputable worldwide fame. For this is, indeed, the wine made from the vines brought over by Roman armies; the wine praised in the fourth century by the poet and Roman consul Ausonius (also the private tutor of Emperor Gratian), who introduced it to the Caesars' table in Rome. It is also the wine that was poured to celebrate the masses held at our patron saint's hermitage, where many pilgrims gathered and prayed. Finally, it is the very wine that was deemed "nectar of the Gods" by King Louis XIV.

Dissolved in 1789 during the French Revolution, the Jurade was restored in 1948 by Jean Capdemourlin, Daniel Querre, Émile Prot, Count de Carles and several other

Saint-Émilionnais figures, with the help of Abbé Bergey, a Catholic priest who was also their deputy at the National Parliament. A few years later, it was led with great verve by Jean Dubois-Challon, the affable owner of Château Ausone, of whom I had the honour to be the successor. The Jurade, at that time, ruled over the same territory as it does today, and also over a part of the Libourne region. Libourne, indeed, no longer had any administrative power since all its former parishes had become independent rural districts. A recent extension has placed the vineyards of Lussac Saint--Émilion and Puisseguin Saint-Émilion under the Jurade's authority. In 1948 as in 1199, people of good standing were nominated as jurats; the Jurade's self-assigned mission was to rekindle and maintain a search for quality and respect for their craft in Saint-Émilion winemakers, reminding them of the rigorous set of rules that their ancestors followed before them. Once that goal was reached, the Jurade desired to let the world know about it. Thus it was received at the Palais de l'Élysée by Vincent Auriol, the president of the French Republic, before going to London in 1951 to deposit a huge flower wreath at the foot of Richard the Lionheart's statue near Westminster Abbey, as a token of their gratitude. The Jurade was greeted with great pomp and ceremony by the Lord Mayor of London, who, a few years later, entered Saint-Émilion in full ceremonial dress, his mace bearer, sword bearer and a dozen archers from his personal guard walking alongside, to pay homage to the premier jurat I had become in the meantime. The Jurade was also part of the large Bordeaux delegation, which was led by President Jacques Chaban-Delmas and met with great ceremony throughout the United States, from New York City to Los Angeles and in many other cities, including Chicago and San Francisco. Friendly Belgium has also welcomed us quite a few times, as have many other countries — Germany, Scandinavia, Singapore, Japan, China….

In Saint-Émilion, the Jurade has regularly welcomed public figures and celebrities, including most presidents of the French Republic greeted as "protectors of La Jurade", while Her Majesty the Queen of England wrote to inform us that the clauses of the Picquigny treaty* unfortunately prevented her from accepting that title. Whether at intimate ceremonies or at more solemn celebrations — the Jurade Festival in June or the harvest announcement, the *Ban des Vendanges*, in September — the Jurade has greeted many ambassadors from countries who treasure the wines of Saint-Émilion as landmarks of culture and civilization. Some members of the French Academy have also been jurats — for instance Maurice Druon, a permanent secretary at the Academy who loved our landscapes so much that he settled there, in the Abbaye de Faize. The Jurade has also included great figures of finance (like the US Treasury Secretary), of industry, of commerce; lawyers and doctors, musicians, actors, journalists, and all sorts of celebrities from every continent. Thus, both intimately or ceremoniously, the Jurade has introduced Saint-Émilion and its winemakers to the world.

Thierry Manoncourt
First jurat of Saint-Émilion
(1965–1988)

* A treaty signed in 1475 by kings Louis XI of France
  and Edward IV of England.

THE CLASSIFICATION OF SAINT-ÉMILION

The first classification of Saint-Émilion wines dates back to 1955. No misreading there: It is indeed 1955, not 1855, which is the year of the Médoc and Sauternes classification.

Why are the two classifications so far apart? The answer is quite simple: The 1855 classification was carried out on the occasion of the Paris World Fair by the Bordeaux Chamber of Commerce, whose territorial jurisdiction did not include the Libourne region. Indeed the Libournais was already an economic region in its own right and did not depend on Bordeaux. It had — and still has — its own Wine Traders Union and its own Chamber of Commerce. And since the absence of classification did not harm the Saint-Émilion wines in any way, they carried on with their own development during the end of the nineteenth century and the second half of the twentieth.

However, as time went by, it appeared to the Saint-Émilion wine authorities that a classification would be an extra mark of fame and professionalism for such a great wine region. Thus, as early as 1930, the Wine Traders Union of Saint-Émilion embarked on its creation. The creation of the INAO (the National Institute for Protected Designations of Origin) and the granting of an AOC (Controlled Designation of Origin) to Saint-Émilion wines in 1936 certainly helped the project to take off. As early as 1950, the stress on quality selection was confirmed: A tasting of every vintage was required from all the wines that were submitted for inclusion in the appellation. Furthermore, the Winemakers' Union, in a joint project with the INAO, proposed a classification system. The INAO, which conferred a guarantee of oenological seriousness to the endeavour, agreed to take charge of that classification, which was ruled by a decree dated October 7, 1954.

A REVISION EVERY TEN YEARS

Right from the outset, the rules of the Saint-Émilion classification included a revision every ten years to ensure that consumers, throughout the years, could get a more truthful picture of the situation and that winemakers could monitor quality more closely. The first classification of Saint-Émilion growths, on June 16, 1955 — with the additional laws of August 7 and October 18, 1958 — established a list of twelve First Great Classified Growths and sixty-three Great Classified Growths. The second classification, published on November 17, 1969, superseded the first by adding nine Great Classified Growths to the list. The third classification, officialized on May 23, 1986, included eleven First Great Classified Growths and sixty-three Great Classified Growths. The fourth classification, dated November 8, 1996, included thirteen First Great Classified Growths and fifty-five Great Classified Growths. In 2006, the revision of the classification was cancelled. A decree dated May 14, 2009, valid until after the 2011 harvest, lists seventy-two Classified Growths, fifteen First Great Classified Growths, and fifty-seven Great Classified Growths.

FIRST GREAT CLASSIFIED GROWTHS

A

Château Ausone
Château Cheval Blanc

B

Château Angélus
Château Beauséjour
(*Duffau-Lagarrosse legacy*)
Château Beau-Séjour Bécot
Château Bélair-Monange
Château Canon
Château Figeac
Château La Gaffelière
Château Magdelaine
Château Pavie
Château Pavie Macquin
Château Troplong Mondot
Château TrotteVieille
Clos Fourtet

GREAT CLASSIFIED GROWTHS

Château Balestard La Tonnelle
Château Bellefont-Belcier
Château Bellevue
Château Bergat
Château Berliquet
Château Cadet Bon
Château Cadet-Piola (Giraud-Bélivier)
Château Canon La Gaffelière
Château Cap de Mourlin
Château Chauvin
Château Corbin
Château Corbin Michotte
Château Dassault
Château Destieux
Château Faurie de Souchard
Château Fleur Cardinale
Château Fonplégade
Château Fonroque

Château Franc Mayne
Château Grand Corbin
Château Grand Corbin-Despagne
Château Grand Mayne
Château Grand Pontet
Château Guadet
Château Haut-Corbin
Château Haut-Sarpe
Château L'Arrosée
Château La Clotte
Château La Couspaude
Château La Dominique
Château La Marzelle
Château La Serre
Château La Tour du Pin
(formerly La Tour du Pin Figeac
Moueix)
Château La Tour du Pin Figeac
Château La Tour Figeac
Château Laniote
Château Larcis Ducasse
Château Larmande
Château Laroque
Château Laroze
Château Le Prieuré
Château Les Grandes Murailles
Château Matras
Château Monbousquet
Château Moulin du Cadet
Château Pavie Decesse
Château Petit Faurie de Soutard
Château Ripeau
Château Saint-Georges Côte Pavie
Château Soutard
Château Tertre Daugay
Château Villemaurine
Château Yon Figeac
Clos de L'Oratoire
Clos des Jacobins
Clos Saint-Martin
Couvent des Jacobins

INTRODUCTION

THE SPIRIT
OF A PLACE

Any wine lover visiting the Saint-Émilionnais for the first time will not fail to be seduced by the exceptional beauty of the scenery: plateaux, small valleys, four thousand five hundred hectares of vineyards scattered with gardens, châteaux, Romanesque churches, megalithic monuments — and, in the middle of all that, on a limestone height, a fortified medieval city dominated by one of the highest steeples in the Gironde.

The origins of this generous wine region read like a fairy tale. Before the Christian era, the classified growths of Saint-Émilion were water springs, celebrated for their medicinal virtues. They could cure illnesses of the eyes, lips or stomach, help with amorous encounters and the conception of handsome babies. Four of these famous springs still remain: in the former Saint-Émilion harbour; in the Saint-Émilion hermitage; and on the hills of Pavie and Ferrand. According to some medieval troubadours, the springs had a fairy godmother: the radiant moon deity known as Lucine or Mélusine. She magically made water spring from the rocks and bubble onto the surface of the earth; she scattered giant rocks over the land to create her favourite gardens. Most have disappeared, but some places called Pey or Peyre ("stone") testify to their existence. Besides, they have not all disappeared. A block of limestone, still planted near the antique medicinal spring of the Saint-Émilion harbour, has stood against all hardships. The five-meter-high Pierrefitte standing stone is still honoured by winemakers.

THE BOOK OF HEAVEN: A JOURNEY TO THE ORIGINS

The real story of this standing stone is no less wonderful that the legend attached to it. Some two thousand five hundred years BC, at the time when the pharaohs were building the pyramids of Egypt, Phoenician and Cretan merchants sailed along the west coast of Europe for pewter, a metal much needed by Mediterranean blacksmiths for bronze-making. Pewter happened to be common in Brittany, in Cornwall and in Ireland. Somewhere on the way during their coastal navigation, the Eastern merchants could not fail to spot a sort of inner sea that

THE MENHIR
THAT STANDS CLOSE
TO THE SAINT-ÉMILION
HARBOUR, THE WATER SPRING
AND THE HERMITAGE ARE,
STILL TODAY, A GATHERING
PLACE FOR PILGRIMS.

was actually the enticing estuary of the Garonne, known as Gironde. When the tide of the Atlantic reverses the river's flow, it becomes easy to sail upstream as far as sixty miles inland. And the place that would become Saint-Émilion, with waters teeming with fish, forests rich in game, a mild microclimate and welcoming natives, must have seemed a haven to them. However, they did not come empty-handed themselves, bringing barley, wheat, goats and sheep and teaching the natives the arts of agriculture and cattle-rearing, yet unknown in the region. In order to convey the notion that nature's cycles were intricately linked to planets and the cycle of seasons, they founded a school of technical and practical studies where disciples, with much devotion, learned to read the Book of Heaven: the courses of the Moon, Sun and stars.

From the limestone cliff, which reminded the newcomers of similar materials they used back home, they extracted monumental stones — menhirs and dolmens

— and carried them miles away to mark their meeting places. These monuments proved to be astronomical observatories as well as sanctuaries, and the secular and the religious world were made inseparable in that sacred space. The celestial observers, who were given the status of magis, were endowed with the task of studying the divine laws in order to apply them to earthly life and secure the perpetuation of the world's. They taught the locals how to live in harmony with the stars, nature and animals, and their message appealed to many generations to come. The menhir that stands close to the Saint-Émilion harbour, the water spring and the hermitage are, still today, a gathering place for pilgrims.

Fifteen centuries later, when the Celts reached Aquitaine, they too revered it as a mythical site. Shortly before the Christian era, the Romans upheld this tradition; as did the Wisigoths around 450 AD and finally their enemies and conquerors, the Franks, after 507. Even the Catholic clergy paid respect to the Stone, going so far as to erect a chapel above the former pagan hermitage in the sixteenth century. Until the French Revolution, the pilgrimage to the standing stone continued to grow in importance. The Republic deprived it of a little of its prestige, but not significantly so. When the local farmers became winemakers and strove to harmonize the energies of Heaven and Earth, they were only reviving the old tradition.

HEAVEN, EARTH AND CELESTIAL HARMONY: THE FIRST VINEYARDS

Sometime between 4000 and 2000 BC, a magic creeping vine from the Caucasus named *Vitis vinifera* conquered the Middle East. At the turn of the sixth century BC, the Greeks introduced it to the Gauls, and that was the start of a spectacular evolution. Half a century before the Christian era, Julius Caesar was indignantly describing the Gauls who unabashedly drank pure wine without the addition of water. The Romans, indeed, were more inclined toward cocktail drinking. One of their drink recipes was based on briefly cooked grape must infused with pitch, black pepper, spices, juniper berries, bay leaves, powdered marble, plaster, sea water or honey. The preparation was scalded and caramelized using a red-hot iron, then poured into amphorae, which were stored on the top shelves of smoky kitchens or under sun-heated tiled roofs, until, eventually, their contents were poured into goblets, mixed with water, and served.

Unlike the Gauls, who took an instant liking to pure, unadulterated wine. They planted new grape varieties, including the frost-resistant *Allobrogica* and the humidity-withstanding *Biturica*. They invented the iron-bound wooden barrel. Their vineyards extended into the entire four provinces known as Galliae. In the year 92 AD, Roman emperor Domitian tried to lay an embargo on "Barbarian wine", but the stubbornness of discerning patricians who insisted on getting their nectars from Bordeaux, Burgundy or Mosel soon made the law obsolete. In the fourth century, the famous poet Ausonius — whose memory is still worshipped in Saint-Émilion — proconsul of Aquitaine and prefect of Italy, Africa and Gaul, claimed that his wine of Lucaniacus (which, legend has it, was made on the spot where the châteaux Ausone and La Gaffelière stand today) was more famous in Rome than the city of Bordeaux itself.

According to a local tradition, the most decisive wine-related event had happened a few years earlier than Ausonius's report — about 280 AD. By decree of Emperor Marcus Aurelius Probus, some centurions

THE LEADER ADVISED
THEM TO TRADE
THEIR SWORD FOR A PLOUGH,
AND THEIR CLUB FOR
AN ACTUAL VINE PLANT.

were requested to retire. The leader advised them to trade their sword for a plough, and their club — which, as a sign of their belonging to an elite corps, was carved from a vine stock — for an actual vine plant. Some soldiers accepted the deal and soon farmers from the fertile Dordogne valley, at the foot of the Saint-Émilion hills, were surprised to see some crazy Romans climbing up the cliff. Once at the top, they carved long parallel furrows set one foot apart, filled them with soil and planted grape vines into them. This balcony-type viticulture was originally practised in Byzantium, and some examples of it are still visible in Great Classified Growth plots on the limestone promontory. Contacts between Rome and the Byzantine world were frequent, and young Roman

soldiers most likely learned that art on such occasions.

At that time, much of the commercial trade between Rome and Gaul was carried along the road known as Via Aemiliana, which ran through the region of Emilia. This has given birth to a not entirely illogical hypothesis concerning the origin of the Saint-Émilion name: Perhaps some "crazy Emilians" impressed the local farmers' memories to the point of leaving their name to a place, hitherto considered barren, where they had managed to grow a vineyard with remarkable success. In the eighth century AD, a Christian hermit from Brittany turned Benedictine monk who had some notion of standing stones — the strongest concentration of megaliths worldwide being found in his native region — and also, most probably, some notion of altar wine, decided to build a hermitage in the heart of this fertile land, in a secluded cave from which flows one of the local medicinal springs that were revered in ancient times for their fertility-giving powers. Such was the charisma of this newcomer that pilgrims would climb to the Pierrefitte menhir on the hilltop to visit him. Even after his death, which occurred in 767, the pilgrimage continued, and from the ninth to the eleventh century the sanctuary was extended. Catacombs and an underground chapel were first carved under the hermitage, followed by the extraordinary, cathedral-sized Monolith Church. In the twelfth century, when the name Saint-Émilion appeared for the first time in written sources, nobody knew whether it referred to the hermit's actual name or to a possible nickname. What matters most is that the name depicts both a sacred place and a great vineyard, both governed by the principle of harmony between Heaven and Earth such as it was taught by the well-inspired travellers of the Megalithic era.

SEEKING THE HOLY GRAIL,
REACHING FOR
THE MASTERPIECE: THE RISE OF
SAINT-ÉMILION
IN THE TWELFTH CENTURY

The twelfth century was a period of unprecedented cultural blooming. Through renewed contact with the East, the West discovered — or rediscovered — the Greek philosophy of Plato and Aristotle, but also Persian poetry, Hermetic philosophy, alchemy, Kabbalah and so on. The libraries of Catholic monasteries were brimming with manuscripts eagerly studied by scholars. Under the impulse of Saint Bernard of Clairvaux, the ancient myths of the Celtic oral tradition — mainly the story of Arthur and the Knights of the Round Table — were adapted to Christianity and carried all over Europe by bards in the north and by troubadours in the south. In the same period, stone-cutters, carpenters, cartwrights and potters gathered into highly structured corporate unions in search of perfection. Europe was ready for a new century: the era of the Cathedrals.

The quest for the Holy Grail on a spiritual level and the quest for the masterpiece on an artistic level merged into the metaphoric search of the times, through individual effort towards enlightenment and altruistic love. Monasteries and pilgrimages blossomed all over the continent. The quest for the masterpiece was a search to find fulfilment of the human soul through the excellence of manual activity practised by both agricultural workers and craftsmen, spritually united under that principle. Saint-Émilion was part of the experience. Canons in the Collegial Church and in the Monolith Church, Franciscan monks at the Cordelier Cloister, Dominicans at the Jacobin Cloister, soldier monks at the Commandery, all endowed

with an age-old experience and a no-nonsense farmer philosophy, joined forces to work on the creation of a model city.

A long, thick surrounding wall was built in local limestone to discourage common assailants. The more serious assailants, whom no wall ever stops, were equally subdued by two of the most brilliant arts mastered by the people of Saint-Émilion: word and wine. Two irresistible spells. In the twelfth century, the great migrations were over but dynastic fights between the crowns of England and France threatened the city and its twelve thousand inhabitants. The *prud'hommes*, or "wise men", of Saint-Émilion, were so skilled at negotiating that they obtained the same privileges from the two opposing crowns. For instance, around 1190, Duchess Eleanor of Aquitaine and her son Richard the Lionheart both granted to Saint-Émilion the status of free town, governed by jurats, city representatives elected on a yearly basis. With the exception of the rights to recruit an army and to mint coins, they had all the power of a local government.

Even the Hundred Years' War, in the fourteenth and fifteenth centuries, and the French Wars of Religion in the sixteenth, did not prevent the monarchs of either kingdom from confirming and securing that precious status. Of course, as chroniclers did not fail to point out, such good relationships were helped by generous shipments of wine barrels sent either to the Tower of London or to the Louvre in Paris. This was a good preparation for the development of wine commerce, which already looked promising at the time, and a strategy that helped the jurats to keep their city's cultural identity intact.

Another art was tirelessly practised in Saint-Émilion: alchemy, one of the most secret speculations of Christendom — the art of transmuting lowly matter into noble substances. This philosophy aiming at spiritual fulfilment (the quest for the Holy Grail) through the accomplishment of a perfect work (the quest for the masterpiece) was refined by fifteen centuries of learning and experience. Its Christian followers included priests, bishops and even popes. However, during the Crusades, political power and Church power joined forces, claimed

FROM THE LATE
TWELFTH CENTURY
TO THE EIGHTEENTH,
ON MORE THAN ONE
OCCASION, THEY PAINTED
OR SCULPTED OUTLANDISH
SYMBOLS IN THE MONOLITH
CHURCH.

exclusive rights on the Truth and unanimously disapproved both the alchemist's solitary quest in his secret laboratory and the hermit's mystical meditation in his secluded hermitage. From then on, alchemists were forced to pursue their search in secrecy and communicated in coded language. From the late twelfth century to the eighteenth, they regularly painted or sculpted outlandish symbols in the Monolith Church and in the Collegial Church to sum up the basic principles of their teachings. When you remember that turning grape juice into wine is a form of alchemical transmutation, it is not unreasonable to assume that the Saint-Émilion alchemists played an important part in the perfecting of viticultural techniques. One of them, Jean d'Espagnet, a president of the Bordeaux Parliament who wrote the book Miroir de l'alchimie in 1602, became famous enough to give his name to a Saint-Émilion vineyard.

HUMANISM, REALISM: FROM RENAISSANCE TO MODERN TIMES

It is nevertheless true that the man who became the patron saint of Saint-Émilion winemakers was not an alchemist. And the great patron saints of viticulture, namely Saint Vincent and Saint Martin, were not granted that distinction either. Saint-Émilion chose Saint Valéry (formerly known as Walaric), an austere man from the

lands of Auvergne who, in the sixth century, became the disciple of an even more austere Irish monk, Saint Columba. When he was entrusted with the community's garden, he turned it into a verdant paradise. According to a chronicle, "his orchards were like the earthly manifestation of a heavenly blessing". After his death in 622, the city of Saint-Valéry-sur-Somme was founded around his convent. Things could have remained as they were. But in 1066, William the Conqueror claimed that he owed his victory over the English to Saint Valéry. That was the start, among the local noblemen, of a fierce chase for the relics of "Valiant Valéry" that lasted until 1197 when the boldest of them, Richard the Lionheart, grabbed the whole reliquary chest, dealing its "treasures" bit by bit to each monastery he wished to honour.

That is probably how the "dear and loyal vassals of Saint-Émilion", shortly after their city had been granted a free town status by Richard the Lionheart, came into possession of a relic of Saint Valéry and placed it near the hermit Saint Émilion's wall-niche tomb. Saint Valéry's reputation as a great Benedictine gardener was still remembered. He became dear to the heart of Saint-Émilion winemakers, who took him as their patron saint. His figure may be admired on a sixteenth-century carefully chiselled painted statue, in full winemaker's dress, ready to accomplish his magnum opus: the classification of Saint-Émilion vineyards. The gardener saint was preferred to the warrior saint. Once again, ancient wisdom held peace higher than war.

The long history of the Saint-Émilion wine appellation is the expression of a definite lifestyle, a subtle mix of humanism and realism that was remarkably analysed by philosophers Montaigne and Montesquieu, both of them Aquitaine-born. It is no coincidence that, in 1794, during the French Revolutionary Terror, the homes and underground quarries of Saint-Émilion were the hiding place of moderate Republicans of the Girondine party, fleeing from the extremist militia of the Montagnard party. In

1884, overwhelmed by the devastation brought by phylloxera and mildew, the Saint-Émilion winemakers once again demonstrated their solidarity and practical mind by creating the first winemakers' union of France, a distant legacy of medieval corporations. In 1935, they played a crucial part in the creation of the INAO, the National Institute for Designation of Origins. They devoted the same fervour to the creation, in 1948, of the Comité Interprofessionnel des Vins de Bordeaux, which grouped winemakers and wine traders together. That very same year, they restructured the Jurade, which had been terminated by the Revolutionary Convention. Their intention was to define quality standards that would allow others to gain the same level of notoriety as the greatest châteaux in order to promote Saint-Émilion wines worldwide.

The quest for the masterpiece goes on: During the last decades, the winemakers have allowed new experiences in viticulture and oenology into the wine châteaux, while remaining attached to their cultural heritage. This balance of history and innovation has led to the classification, in 1999, of the entire Saint-Émilion vineyard as a World Heritage Site — a first in the history of UNESCO. The decision paid homage to the pure water springs that have been worshipped there since ancient times. Every ten years, the Great Classified Growths revise their classification, while many generations of artists and craftsmen — probably inspired by the spirit of Saint Valéry — come from far and wide to help the Saint-Émilion vineyards to remain "the earthly manifestation of a heavenly blessing". Last but not least, the UNESCO decision pays tribute to the forever young, radiant entity that permeates the whole Saint-Émilionnais: the spirit of the place.

FIRST GREAT CLASSIFIED GROWTHS OF SAINT-ÉMILION

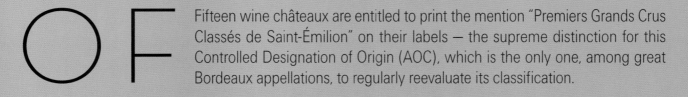

Fifteen wine châteaux are entitled to print the mention "Premiers Grands Crus Classés de Saint-Émilion" on their labels — the supreme distinction for this Controlled Designation of Origin (AOC), which is the only one, among great Bordeaux appellations, to regularly reevaluate its classification.

CHÂTEAU
CHEVAL BLANC

This prestigious vineyard is one of the two First Great Saint-Émilion A Classified Growths — a distinction it shares with Ausone — as well as one of the most famous wines in the world. Cheval Blanc was created in 1832, when Henriette Ducasse, daughter of President Ducasse, married Jean Fourcaud-Laussac, a wine trader from Libourne. As a dowry, she brought him ten hectares in a place called Cheval-Blanc, south of Château L'Évangile, on a lovely terroir to the northwest of Saint-Émilion. During the following decades, a clever land-buying policy led to the creation of a beautiful estate. Cheval-Blanc acquired its final shape in 1971 — forty-one hectares including thirty-six hectares of vines. The perimeter has not been modified since then.

During the nineteenth century, the Libourne wine trader set out to embellish the architectural elements of the estate as well. He extended the existing farm, raising it by one floor, adding a turret, a chapel, a glass canopy over the front door and finally an orangery. He also designed a garden and laid out lawns before the front steps. A true fairy-tale castle, delicate and refined, almost feminine, rose from the ground, quite different from the sturdy Girondine mansions around. Then, when he started working on the vineyard, he found out that the local

Right: Pierre Lurton, general manager.

type of clay was perfectly adapted to cabernet franc, which he subsequently planted on two-thirds of the thirty-six hectares, thus imparting roundness, elegance and aromatic complexity to his wine. To such an extent that he decided to change its name, "vin de Figeac", to "Cheval Blanc", taking inspiration from an old legend stating that King Henry IV once slept in an inn that used to stand there. The thankful innkeeper had — so they say — renamed his house after the French king's famous white horse.

At the end of the nineteenth century, Cheval Blanc was praised and prized at all international fairs, and was classified as a First Great Growth in 1955. Jean Fourcaud-Laussac's descendants, gathered into a professional partnership between the two world wars, went on running the property for seventy years until they became too numerous and the sale of the family treasure to two businessmen, Albert Frère and Bernard Arnault, was concluded.

Today, Château Cheval Blanc has the reputation of being one of the most reliable wines in the world, whatever the vintage. Pierre Lurton — its indefatigable general manager for nearly twenty years, a father of six and a lover of antique sailing ships (he is also the manager of Château d'Yquem, another prestigious property of the Frère-Arnault team) — tells the story: "Cheval Blanc has a cashmere texture. It is the epitome of durable elegance."

No fewer than a hundred events are held at Cheval Blanc each year, most of them in the orangery and in the recently renovated tasting room where terracotta tiles, orange walls, grey arcades, designer tasting tables and huge vases of white orchids make up a sumptuous reception space. While not inhabited on a regular basis, the château, built on a human scale, still keeps a few bedrooms for important guests and famous collectors from all over the world who wish to visually experience the birthplace of their favourite nectar. On the ground floor, you may see a small kitchen replete with jars of jams and preserves, and some reception rooms. A corridor opens out into a cellar, soon to be entirely redesigned by architect Christian de Portzamparc, who has conceived a state-of-the-art inner space with a double-helix staircase and a landscaped garden that, he guarantees, will fit to perfection into Cheval Blanc's classic, refined setting. To be discovered in 2011.

CHÂTEAU
ANGÉLUS

Hubert de Boüard de Laforest remembers that long ago, winemakers used to taste the soil from the vineyard to verify its quality. He contents himself with inhaling it at daybreak, with his dogs alongside him. "Smelling the vineyard" is a ritual accomplished by seven generations of Boüards at Angélus, an illustrious family property facing full south, on the Saint-Émilion *pied de côte*. This amphitheatre-shaped setting, less than a mile away from the village, used to reverberate to the sound of the angelus bells from the three neighbouring churches, hence the name. When Hubert and his cousin Jean-Bernard Grenié took over Château Angélus in 1985, he found it perfectly sensible to move with his wife and their four children into the house where his ancestors were born — an eighteenth-century former hunting lodge built in the sturdy Girondine style, with hip roofs and a porch opening out directly onto the vineyard. Long ago, the vines brushed against the house porch, but Hubert's grandmother insisted on doing away with a few precious vine stocks and replacing them with an ornamental garden from which a landscape of almost Tuscan gentleness could be enjoyed — the roofs of Château Magdelaine, the cypresses and the church steeples. And now, beyond the kitchen, a terrace planted with lemon trees, a swimming pool and an orchard.

Left: Hubert de Boüard de Laforest and his cousin Jean-Bernard Grenié.

Few traces of the past remain in the house aside from the family crest carved in stone above the mantelpiece. Instead, dozens of contemporary paintings hang on the walls or simply lean onto them: a piano, a library devoted to cigar-related books — another one of the owner's passions — and the pictures of many wine-loving celebrities, movie stars and politicians who have come to enjoy Angélus's peaceful atmosphere and share a good bottle. Indeed, from the day when seven-year-old Hubert grabbed his first pair of winemaking shears to his later days as president of the winemakers' union, then to his current position as chairman of the Groupement des Premiers Grands Crus Classés, he has focused on one single purpose: extending the course of history, opening out to the world, and sharing his experience through teaching. "Wine is great only when it leads people to another dimension," he says. For instance to contemporary art, to which a passionate Hubert de Boüard is planning to dedicate a portion of his antique cellars.

CHÂTEAU
BEAUSÉJOUR

Owned by the Duffau-Lagarosse family since 1847, Beauséjour is one of the few First Great Classified Growths of Saint-Émilion to be managed by a family-run company, created in 1963. Today, no fewer than thirty heirs attend the company meetings to discuss the estate's destiny. The property is managed by two of their cousins, Christophe Redaud and Vincent Duffau-Lagarosse.

To reach the château, you need to climb uphill to the small Saint-Martin church. You will discover, leaning on its walls, a lovely blonde stone mansion built on a promontory. From its terrace, the panoramic view is breathtaking: the isthmus of the Dordogne, the surrounding vineyards and dovecotes, and even, on a clear night, the distant lights of Bordeaux. Down below, a small shady park overlooks the road leading to Libourne. The remains of an old wash-house may still be seen, but only the eldest are likely to remind the children that the beautiful lawn they now see used to be a paddock for the workhorse who helped on the vineyard. The estate, which formerly included Beau-Séjour Bécot, now covers seven hectares. Here, too, the limestone, pierced through by

many stone quarries, is a convenient shelter for nearly thirty thousand bottles. Each room, each detail of the house is a reminder of the many generations who have lived there and made Beauséjour a Saint-Émilion landmark. The family members stay connected through this old family home. Indeed all the Duffau-Lagarosses, extremely devoted to the vineyard and to their own roots, share a common wish to preserve and embellish the aptly named Château Beauséjour so that their children may enjoy it for many years to come.

Below: Vincent Duffau-Lagarosse, comanager of Château Beauséjour SC.

CHÂTEAU
BEAU-SÉJOUR BÉCOT

The Bécots are a family who seriously care about wine: Michel, the father, Dominique and Gérard, his two sons, lovers of nature, hunting and fine wines; and Gérard's daughter, the irresistible Juliette, who considers it her duty to promote the family's wines, and above all this First Great Growth, throughout the world. Located at the heart of the appellation, on the plateau of Saint-Martin de Mazerat, west of the village, Beau-Séjour Bécot has been devoted to winemaking since ancient Roman times. Eighteen and a half hectares in area, the estate currently belongs to the Bécots, a family who has been making wine in Saint-Émilion for twelve generations. "Long ago, vineyard owners used to have an additional job or extra income. My grandfather was also a draper and my father used to sell automobile spare parts. I was the first one to make my entire living from the vine," says Gérard. Now, each member of the family has their own house on the estate with a view over the vineyard from the early hours of the day.

When Michel, in 1985, gave the property over to his sons, Gérard was thirty-five and Beau-Séjour Bécot, because its surface had increased, had just been "downgraded" as a Great Classified Growth, thus losing its position in the high-class

Facing page, top left: Gérard Bécot and his daughter Juliette.

First Growths Management Group. In 1979, Michel had decided to unite Beau-Séjour and his neighbouring vineyards, La Carte and Trois Moulins, which benefited from the same terroir and the same exceptional planting, but he had to show proof that he had done the right thing. "My father told me: 'You have ten years to be a First Growth again.'" A challenge that was brilliantly met by the family in 1996, through careful respect of nature and the terroir, the use of traditional skills and of innovative techniques handed down by each generation.

After showing us the beautiful rotunda-shaped tasting room, Gérard takes us through the strange quarries that were used as an ossuary for the Saint-Émilion graveyard and still lead into Château Canon. When he passionately describes barrel-making and the origin of woods, which are heated according to his own instructions, he makes you grasp the reality of a winemaker's life. "I praise my father for giving me the property when I was still a young man. My only daughter, Juliette, used to work in film distribution. One day, in autumn, she came over for the grape harvest and never left. I gave her half of my shares, as my father had done for me." The Bécots certainly know something about transmission.

CHÂTEAU
BÉLAIR-MONANGE

A Premier Grand Cru Classé of exceptional fame, Château Bélair was already bottled at the château as early as 1802. Property of the Dubois-Challon family in the twentieth century, since 2008 it has belonged to the Etablissements Jean-Pierre Moueix, who added the name Monange as a tribute to Adèle Monange, the first woman of the Moueix family to arrive in Saint-Émilion back in the 1930s. Her great-grandson, Edouard Moueix, has decided to entirely renovate the vineyard as well as the château, a genuine architectural curiosity, where he intends to live. The history of Saint-Émilion is contained in the stone walls of Bélair-Monange. Originally English, the vineyard belonged to Sir Robert Knolles, governor of Guyenne in the fourteenth century. It remained the property of his heirs when, one century later, after Charles V conquered the province, they settled in the estate and Gallicized its name into "cru de Canolle", before it became Bélair.

On top of a steep hill, at the highest point of the plateau where vines have grown since Roman times, as is testified by the limestone furrows discovered on the twelve-and-a-half hectare vineyard, this ancient military or religious site dominates the valley and surrounding hills for seven miles around. The road leading to it, as if carved into the rock with a single blow of an ax, surprises any visitor. The constructions

prior to the delicate Renaissance château are the witness of Saint-Émilion's history. Originally troglodytic, year after year houses were carved into the limestone, of which important blocks can still be seen emerging from the façade. The small sixteenth-century château, with its elegant dove-grey shutters, a pavilion overlooking the plain, and a chapel also carved in the rock, is in the Mansard style typical of the nearby Dordogne region. In spite of an intimate appearance, four levels of underground quarries, the largest in Saint-Émilion, stretch behind Bélair-Monange, hosting extensive cellars. Endless, impressive tunnels lead through a spiral staircase to the collection of bottles from old vintages. A dream of a little château where you could, just like Édouard, easily picture yourself living.

Facing page: Édouard Moueix, manager.

CHÂTEAU
CANON

When frigate lieutenant Jacques Kanon, a privateer for the king of France, purchased the estate with his perilously earned fortune in the eighteenth century, he most probably built some of his own elegance and proud appearance into the chartreuse. Lemon trees framing the front steps in the main courtyard; delicate, aerial wrought iron; a peculiar-looking square tower built in more recent times, covered in Virginia creeper and wisteria — and the famous blue, the same worn by the jockeys of the Wertheimer stables, applied everywhere in discreet but decided touches. In 1996, the three brothers fell in love with Château Canon, whose wall-enclosed twenty-two hectares of vineyards are now part of the Chanel real-estate assets.

Next to the small Saint-Martin church, whose thin steeple seems to float above the surrounding vines, the château's façade conceals a lovely enclosed garden with green laurel arcades, the soothing shade of two large holm oaks, a small vegetable garden and gently swaying hollyhocks. No wonder that this graceful, appealing chartreuse seduced John Kolasa, a buoyantly bearded Scotsman who became the manager of Château Canon after having done just about every wine-related job. A passionate advocate of *vins de garde*, striding through the now uninhabited château, he loves to describe

the daily life of the seventeen workers employed on the estate on a permanent basis. Prestigious tastings are held in the enfilade reception rooms, while more intimate dinners are served in the dining room, where the decor includes an imposing Bordelais cupboard and fabrics printed with crimson grapes.

A MAGIC PLACE

The library gives direct access to the barrel cellars, which lead into the sparkling new vathouse, John's personal pride: twenty-four sparkling new stainless steel vats separated by blue pillars. The lighting is subtle and beautiful, revealing the gorgeous roof structure. However, one of the most magical parts of the château is buried underground: huge stone quarries, abandoned since the nineteenth century, stretch in amazing, endless tunnels: eighteen hectares, almost the whole surface of the estate.

Beautifully restored and lit like the cellars above, they are also connected to the underground tunnels of the neighbouring château, Beau-Séjour Bécot. "This is where the heart of Château Canon beats," says John, smiling. "Deep in this limestone core which gives the wine its velvety, silky texture. You know, men come and go — only the terroir remains."

Above: John Kolasa, manager.

CHÂTEAU
DE FIGEAC

The huge park of Château de Figeac seems to be an exception in the Bordelais wine region. For nearly two thousand years, since its creation in the second century AD by the Figeacus family, the estate has retained its peaceful, welcoming family atmosphere. For a long time, the landscape, the vineyard and the architecture bore the mark of the famous Decazes family, then from 1654 to 1838 they were followed by the Carles, a famous name in political as well as in viticultural history. Since 1892, the Manoncourt family has been at the head of the property.

A trained agricultural engineer, Thierry Manoncourt is one of the most respected men in the region. He was the first winemaker in the Bordelais to put his scholarly knowledge of malolactic fermentation into practice. His inquisitive mind led him to much experimenting. In 1970, he built a huge extra barrel cellar opening out onto the vineyard and dug deep underground cellars in order to perform gravitational bottling, earning the nickname of "Saint-Émilion Pharaoh" in the local press. More importantly, he opened the estate to the public very early on. He is also one of the three founding members of the Union des Grands Crus de Bordeaux. In 1988, Thierry and Marie-France Manoncourt proposed to Laure, one of their four daughters, and to her husband Count Éric d'Aramon, to join them. They are the current managers of the family estate, while Thierry and Marie-France love to welcome children,

Left: Count Éric d'Aramon, general manager.

grandchildren and friends in the renovated central aisle of the château.

Located to the west of Saint-Émilion, next to the greatest Pomerols, the Figeac vineyard lies on an exceptional gravelly terroir that earned it the title of First Great Classified Growth. At Figeac, the vineyard leaves space for the garden. All parts of the estate are cared for with the same attention to detail and respect for the environment. Thus the property ages beautifully and adds a precious contribution to history. Here and there the soothing touches of a medieval dovecote, a wing of the château, a tower, Renaissance pillars or a few mullioned windows appear to the eye. The main wing offers the pure and elegant lines of an eighteenth-century façade overlooking a lovely courtyard. In the nineteenth century, one of the wings was extended and completed with a huge terrace overlooking the lower courtyard, the vegetable garden and the surrounding landscape. In 2010, antique stables were converted into state-of-the-art offices and large new farm buildings were built, but research is also practised on the replanting of ancient hedge varieties.

Sometimes, on winter weekends, as a relief from promotional dinners all over the world, the family gathers in the impressive, copper-adorned kitchen where, every morning, a baker leaves bread while a milkman drops off fresh raw milk and newly laid eggs. More formal parties comprising about twenty diners are held in the dining room whose walls are lit up by a peacock-patterned eighteenth-century wallpaper. In the summertime, the whole family gathers for holiday leisure under the pergola overlooking the gardens, the pond, the woods, the tennis court and the swimming pool.

A warm advocate of oenotourism, the family welcomes thousands of visitors every year and renovates the old winemakers' houses. As you discover the huge tasting room — a hundred square meters between carved stone walls — and its monumental mantelpiece, you easily understand that Figeac is truly devoted to history, wine, refinement and hospitality.

CHÂTEAU
LA GAFFELIÈRE

Just push open the gates of Château La Gaffelière and watch the magic in action. Twenty-two hectares of vineyards, all in the same lot, tucked in between the prestigious hills of Ausone and Pavie; a massive seventeenth- and eighteenth-century mansion, remodelled in the nineteenth century in the neogothic fashion; a park — almost a botanical garden — laid out by its owner Count de Malet Roquefort; a pond, and two bronze horses grazing on the lawn. For four centuries, the Malet Roqueforts — the oldest family in the village, in the centre of which their original house may still be seen — have tied their destiny to that of the Saint-Émilion vines. A family of soldiers and landowners (many of whom were at times mayor of the town), they always took the utmost care of this family house and of its illustrious vineyard. For fifty years, therefore, Léo de Malet Roquefort has watched over the destiny of La Gaffelière. A father of five, an expert horseman, fond of hunting and Bugattis, this winemaker endowed with a deep aesthetic sense inhabits today the estate where his ancestors were born. He has already prepared his son Alexandre to take it over someday.

On the death of his father, in 1958, Léo had to leave for

Above: Léo de Malet Roquefort, owner, and his son Alexandre.

Algeria and had no choice but to manage the property at a distance as well as he could, through letters and telegrams sent to his sister and his devoted vineyard master. He who dreamed of being an electrical engineer became a winemaker. Back in France, he learned the art of inter-vine stock ploughing using a horse, and of making and selling wine; he selected a team of renowned experts so that La Gaffelière remained among the greatest wines in the world. One foot in the vineyard, the other one in art, he enthusiastically leads visitors into the château where ancient artefacts match his own taste in perfect harmony, confessing his passion for Bordeaux furniture, French Regency style, wildlife bronze sculpture and any wine-related form of art. On the way, he shows them the magnificent vaulted fifteenth-century kitchen where winter dinners are served, with its Gothic-style mantelpiece and stone kitchen sink; the *grand salon* complete with a connoisseur's choice of ancient paintings; the seventeenth- and eighteenth-century wings now used as reception rooms; and the vaulted underground barrel cellar supported by an imposing, beautifully lit central pillar. Around the swimming pool, more wonders to see: a summer kitchen with an open-space sitting room and an antique dovecote — now a pool house. In the former cellar converted into guest rooms is a reception room holding up to fifty guests. Indeed La Gaffelière is also a place of celebration; friendly parties or professional events revolving around wine are invariably warm and luxurious, leaving guests with long-lasting happy memories — blame that on Count Léo de Malet's highly contagious joie de vivre.

CHÂTEAU
MAGDELAINE

Well-hidden behind imposing holm oak trees, Château Magdelaine is the most discreet of Saint-Émilion Premiers Grands Crus Classés and, like the site, its wines have the reputation of being the most feminine. Fronted by a small romantic park and its dovecote, the eighteenth-century mansion opens onto the vast Dordogne Valley. In 1850, numerous vineyards bore the name Magdelaine. Only at the end of the nineteenth century did Jean Chatonnet unify them as distinct entities, creating Château Magdelaine, a horse-shoe-shaped vineyard of eleven and a half hectares on the limestone terrace of Saint-Émilion. Acknowledged in 1922 as producing one of the three best wines of the appellation, together with Ausone and Bélair, the vineyard fell into oblivion with the next generation, until it was taken over by Jean-Pierre Moueix in 1952, and classified as a Premier Grand Cru Classé in 1955.

For decades, the old vines on the plateau and the steep south slopes were ploughed by Pompon, the last horse to have worked a vineyard in Saint-Émilion, and whose red-doored stable can still be seen. Every year during autumn,

Magdelaine comes to life when one generation after another of railway workers from the north of France arrives for the harvests. Long tables are then set under the shade of large trees for animated lunches, before the property settles back into its usual tranquility. The Moueix family shall soon renovate this genuine "sleeping beauty", respecting its discreet and sober style, in perfect harmony with the family's philosophy.

Below, left: Christian Moueix, CEO of Établissements Jean-Pierre Moueix.

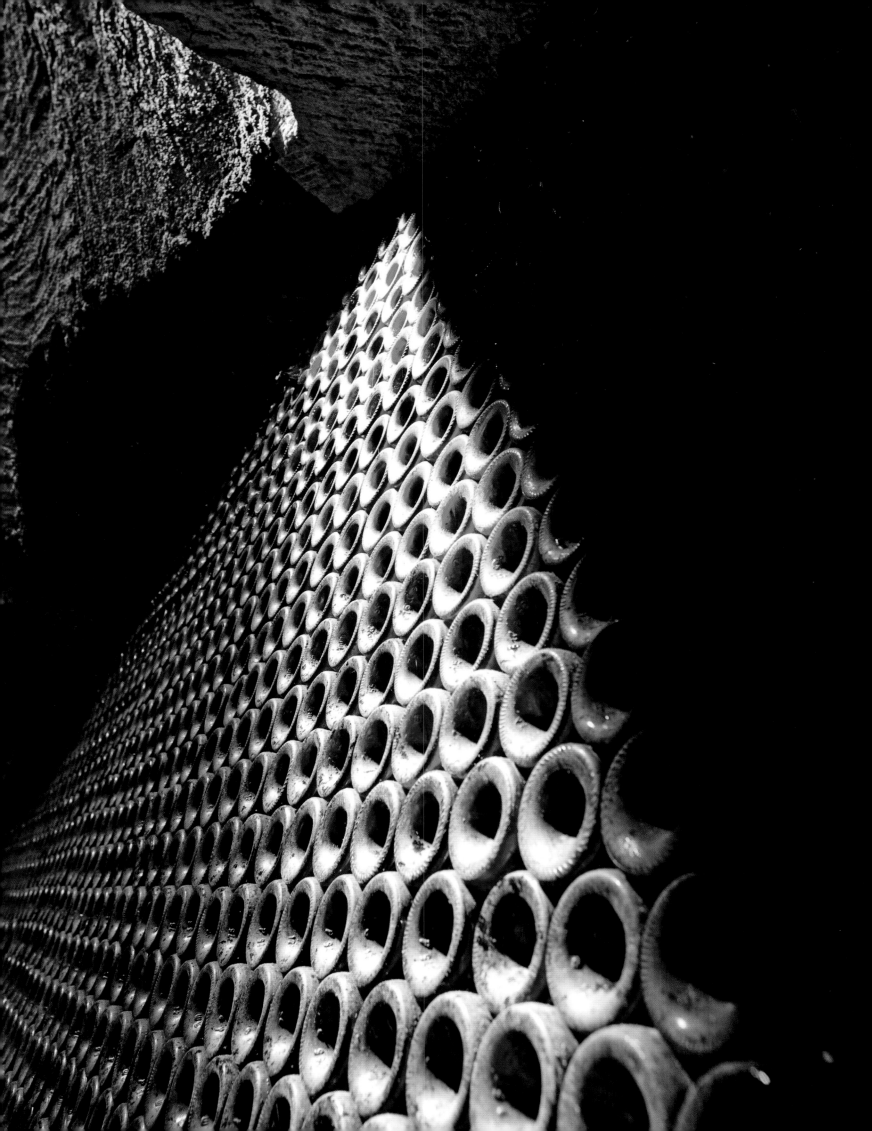

CHÂTEAU
PAVIE

I n America, they love this kind of story: A young man from the Paris suburbs with a passion for wine gets rich through hypermarket distribution, then gives it all up and buys Château Pavie, a First Great Classified Growth, in order to devote himself to the three exceptional terroirs that make up the estate. The forty-hectare all-in-one-piece vineyard, one of the most extensive in the appellation, is also the most dramatically sloping. Approaching the estate from its lowest part on the road, you pass by the cellars and the vines planted on the *pied de côte* before ascending to the château — a large nineteenth-century three-storied mansion — and the *middle-of-côte* plots, then higher still to reach the limestone plateau. Meanwhile, starting from twenty meters above sea level, you have risen to a hundred and ten. No wonder, then, that Gérard Perse does not reside on the property: At Pavie, all you do is climb up and down.

For years, while he was working for supermarkets, Gérard made a point of buying each and every wine himself. To that end, he regularly travelled to the Bordeaux region to meet with winemakers, wine traders and *maîtres de chai* (cellar masters). "They taught me everything," he says. "I studied their winemaking and ageing techniques. It was fascinating." So he fell in love with Saint-Émilion and asked his friends to help him find a vineyard so he could practise his skills. In 1992, he bought Château Monbousquet and put his ideas to the test. All the while, across the road, the Pavie vineyard triggered his daydreams — a wonderful layered terroir of gravel, clay and limestone. In 1998, when he heard Pavie was for sale, he sold all his belongings, bought the estate and had his whole family move to Saint-Émilion. From then on, he turned his handicap of not having been born in the region and lacking a family-inherited wine culture into an asset. Free of any preconceptions and of the weight of tradition, he introduced leaf-stripping, green harvest and yield control.

Top left: Gérard Perse, owner.
Facing page, top right: Jean-Baptiste Pion, *maître de chai*.

Year after year, he improved the blending. His daughter Angélique and her husband gave up their jobs to work with him. Soon, critics enthusiastically described his magnificent vaulted, cathedral-like cellar, with a mezzanine and an archway salvaged from the former Orléans train station in Bordeaux. Soon, however, he will be able to lead them into the tasting room and the reception room — still under construction on the rooftop by designer Alberto Pinto — where art shows and concerts will be held throughout the year.

CHÂTEAU
PAVIE MACQUIN

Standing on the plateau overlooking Saint-Émilion, at an altitude of three hundred feet, the huge oak tree that reigns over the land of Pavie Macquin is easy to spot from miles around. A holm oak to be precise, with a legend attached to it. In ancient times, justice was done in its shade and the tree was nicknamed "the hangman's oak". Such is the meaning of the label on the bottle of Château Pavie Macquin, a wine recently promoted to First Great Classified Growth: two oak leaves, and a rope! This all-in-one-piece fifteen-hectare vineyard, bordering Troplong Mondot to the east, Pavie to the north and TrotteVieille to the south, includes an ancient farmhouse to which new storage cellars and a rather modern-looking tasting room have been added. The most striking part of the ensemble is the vathouse, where each tank bears a woman's name — Gertrude, Fernande, Éliane… How could winemaking ever fail in such good company, with such illustrious neighbours to boot?

The property's "historical" owner, Albert Macquin, was an agricultural engineer who, in the late nineteenth century,

Right: Nicolas Thienpont, manager.

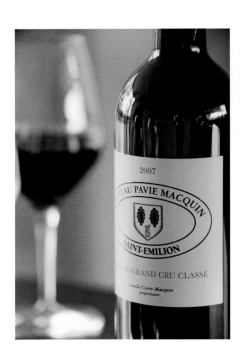

saved the Saint-Émilion vineyard from total ruin by introducing the use of grafted stocks. His children having chosen careers as merchant marines, his grandchildren — the Corre-Macquin family — though scattered in all corners of France, decided to hold on to their ancestor's property and regularly come down for the grape harvest. For the last fifteen years, they have entrusted Nicolas Thienpont with the estate. Nicolas has played a crucial part in the wine's consecration. Indeed, caught between frosts and strokes of mildew, the vineyard was at the end of its tether. "This estate," Thienpont says, "is a great experimental lab. It gave us an opportunity to put in practice some production methods that, since then, have proven their validity in neighboring wine châteaux. Our idea was not to create a new wine but to reveal this Cinderella's true splendour while staying true to nature and to a dynamic tradition. Pavie Macquin is a very powerful wine that needed nothing but a touch of grace." Mission accomplished.

Above: Agricultural engineer Albert Macquin (1852–1911) gave his name to the property. Saint-Émilion owes to him the introduction of grafted planting, which saved the French vineyard after the phylloxeric plague.

ELIANE

HORTENSE

GERTRUDE

IRENE

CHÂTEAU
TROPLONG MONDOT

f any place deserves to be described as the epitome of elegant lifestyle, it is Troplong Mondot. It is also a lively home where Christine and Xavier Pariente, their five daughters and their dog Félix love to welcome visiting friends and professional partners. Indeed, at Troplong Mondot, the attention given to the decor and setting is equal to the care devoted to the great wine. Christine and Xavier are perfect hosts, liberally providing elaborate fare made from the natural products of their orchard, vegetable garden and poultry coop, whether in the family kitchen warmed by the big fireplace or in the dining room overlooking the village of Saint-Émilion.

The history of the estate began in the eighteenth century. The Mondot vineyard belonged at the time to the abbé de Sèze, whose family already owned many other wine estates in the Bordeaux region. He decided to adorn it with the stately and beautiful mansion that is still nestled in a park of century-old oak trees. In 1850, Raymond Troplong, president of the French Senate and *pair de France*, fell in love with the property and increased its surface to its definitive thirty-three hectares. In the early twentieth century, Alexandre Valette, a wine trader and restaurant owner, acquired the property. His great-granddaughter, Christine, aged no more

Left: Christine and Xavier Pariente, owners.

than twenty, took it over in 1980, ten years before she was joined by her husband, Xavier Pariente, an antique dealer specializing in eighteenth-century art. This happy marriage, in 2006, led Troplong Mondot into the prestigious group of First Great Classified Growths; and Xavier, in order to complement his wife's efforts, soon devoted himself entirely to the vineyard and buildings of Troplong Mondot. Thus the cellars and vathouse were restructured at the same time as new and more environmentally friendly growing methods were introduced in the vineyard.

For over fifteen years, Christine and Xavier have been renovating and redecorating the property; antique woodwork and cornices may be seen next to contemporary paintings, or Italian console tables next to Eaves armchairs. The barrel cellar, with its multifaceted crystal chandeliers set in staggered rows and its concrete floor painted with iron oxide, is a must-see; so are the state-of-the-art vathouse with its grey cement floor and black ceiling and the huge reception room with its fireplace — a perfect setting for parties. Troplong Mondot, one should add, is the only remaining château in Saint-Émilion where the harvest is done every year by a group of Gypsies who gather there in their trailers. Such is the life potential of the place that some have even been married on the premises. "There is nothing surprising about that," says Xavier Pariente as he proudly shows us around. "Wine is the expression of a lifestyle and our task is to represent it."

CHÂTEAU
TROTTEVIEILLE

TrotteVieille is the story of love at first sight; or how Marcel Borie, a Bordeaux wine trader, fell in love with the 1943 vintage of Château TrotteVieille and purchased it in its entirety. Such was his emotion as he tasted the wine that he instantly set off for the estate to discover this exceptional terroir, one of the two wine estates in Saint-Émilion — with Ausone — that sits on extremely limited clay and limestone. And that was when the lightning of passion struck again, this time for aesthetic reasons, when he saw the run-down eighteenth-century chartreuse whose name is linked to the legend of a *vieille* (an old lady) who used to *trotter* (toddle) every day to the post office below for fresh news. Marcel Borie bought the whole estate in 1947, having had to sell a few estates in central France to do so.

Today, the charm of TrotteVieille is unspoiled. An alley of century-old horse-chestnut trees leads to an elegant mansion amid ten hectares of wines — a wall-enclosed, all-in-one-piece vineyard from which the whole surrounding region may be admired: Pomerol to the north, then Libourne, Saint-Émilion and its valley, and the Entre-Deux-Mers. Behind the building, a small park planted with cypress and hackberry trees offers a romantic view over the vineyards. Through inheritance, the

Right: Philippe Castéja, administrator.

estate was acquired by the Castéja, a family of Médoc vineyard owners for more than three centuries. In the late 1980s, they passed it on to their heir Philippe with the responsibility of taking it to a top level. Since the 1960s, the house, ruined by successive burglaries, had remained empty. He installed a library — a passion of his father's — and renovated the bedrooms and the park, but his main concern was the vineyard. "After modern technical wine-growing improvements were introduced in the 1960s," Philippe says, "with the later progress of oenological science, the plant itself — the vine — was not seriously studied until the late 1990s. That was when vineplanting and pruning were improved and redefined. Trottevieille has very old vines, planted in one foot of clay spread onto a limestone bedrock. This is what gives the wine its character. We have made use of traditional techniques, with a deeper understanding of their causes. We are lucky to have a small plot planted with prephylloxeric vines. The wine from this plot is made individually and 132 engraved and numbered flasks of it are bottled. The majority goes into Trottevieille Grand Vin. We taste them and the grand vin simultaneously in order to understand and appreciate the latter's evolution. Winemaking is a work of patience," he continues. "The vine needs to be observed and studied for a long time before any change can be brought to its treatment."

CLOS
FOURTET

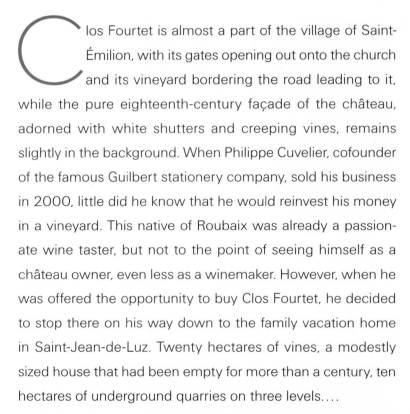

C los Fourtet is almost a part of the village of Saint-
Émilion, with its gates opening out onto the church
and its vineyard bordering the road leading to it,
while the pure eighteenth-century façade of the château,
adorned with white shutters and creeping vines, remains
slightly in the background. When Philippe Cuvelier, cofounder
of the famous Guilbert stationery company, sold his business
in 2000, little did he know that he would reinvest his money
in a vineyard. This native of Roubaix was already a passionate wine taster, but not to the point of seeing himself as a
château owner, even less as a winemaker. However, when he
was offered the opportunity to buy Clos Fourtet, he decided
to stop there on his way down to the family vacation home
in Saint-Jean-de-Luz. Twenty hectares of vines, a modestly
sized house that had been empty for more than a century, ten
hectares of underground quarries on three levels....

Philippe Cuvelier fell in love with the place and the region.
For months, he worked on the house, renovating the floors
and ceilings, as well as the gorgeous ironwork staircase,
while his wife embellished the place with furniture, doors and
woodwork from nearby antique dealers and *brocantes*. The

unity of style is so well achieved that the house looks like it has been furnished this way for decades. Alive again, it feels warm and welcoming. The sales manager of Clos Fourtet is one of Philippe's sons, Mathieu. He lives in Bordeaux but also devotes his time to Château Poujeaux, the second family property. His father comes every two weeks and the four other children stay there regularly at weekends, at harvest time and in the spring.

The visitor is greeted by beautiful antique tapestries hanging in the hallway. The main living room, with a view onto the terrace and the vineyard, is decorated in red, a colour that is also found in light touches in the tan, grey and white decor of the dining room, where family members or special clients are welcomed. In the huge kitchen opening out onto the west wing and dominated by a fireplace, a massive farmhouse table is used for more informal dinners. Another room — wood-panelled in white and grey, a pink toile-de-Jouy chaise longue, matching the curtains — is an invitation to a few moments of rest. Upstairs, five large bedrooms are decorated in the same harmony. The very same refinement and attention to detail are respected throughout the property, as an echo of the wine that is produced there.

Above: Philippe Cuvelier, owner.

GREAT CLASSIFIED GROWTHS OF SAINT-ÉMILION

Hills, plateaux, a mosaic of soils. Homes, châteaux, history-laden interiors, contemporary interior design, nooks and crannies, artifacts, passions, a park, a bench, a great tree, women, men, children, life… Wines with a personal touch. Our wines.

CHÂTEAU
BALESTARD LA TONNELLE

Back in the fifteenth century, the French poet François Villon was already singing the praise of Balestard La Tonnelle in a poem that may now be read on the château's wine label. Balestard was originally a canon of the Saint-Émilion chapter who gave his name to the property. The first thing that catches your eye as you approach Balestard is "La Tonnelle", an old watchtower whose characteristic shape has dominated the Saint-Émilion vineyard for six centuries.

The property is now run by Jacques Capdemourlin. A well-known local figure, he was *premier jurat* of Saint-Émilion and, for many years, at the head of the winemakers' union. Now his son Thierry lends a hand; both father and son share a passion for their vineyard, where they greet friends and visitors from all over the world.

CHÂTEAU
BELLEFONT-BELCIER

AT THE END OF
THE EIGHTEENTH CENTURY,
COUNT LOUIS FRANÇOIS DE
BELCIER CREATED
THE ESTATE AS A STOPOVER
FOR THE KING.

The vineyard of Bellefont-Belcier was planted on the south hill of Saint-Émilion, between Pavie and Larcis Ducasse. The place owes half of its name to a cluster of freshwater springs nearby, Belcier standing for the name of a powerful family of the Bordelais nobility. At the end of the eighteenth century, Count Louis François de Belcier, a secretary to King Louis XVI of France, created the estate as a stopover for the king, but the French Revolution put a brutal end to the project. After many sales and inheritances, in 1889 the château fell into the hands of the Faures, a family of Bordeaux wine traders. Pierre Faure, a brilliant agricultural engineer and the author of many books, built the famous and unique circular vathouse under a magnificent umbrella-shaped wood and metal framework that was reputedly designed by Gustave Eiffel. This miraculously intact work of art is one of the property's most precious treasures.

In 1994, two friends, Jacques Berrebi and Alain Laguillaumie, gave a new start to the dormant vineyard, restructuring twenty hectares and renovating the buildings with great care for the natural style and spirit of the place. Dominique Hébrard joined them in 2004; the three men carried on with their quality improvement policy, hoping to raise the château's quality back to the level of a Saint-Émilion Grand Cru Classé. Their efforts met with success. Bellefont-Belcier was classified, and the château, having recovered its former splendour, has been converted into a lovely guesthouse where both the luxury of modern comfort and the discreet charm of tradition may be enjoyed.

CHÂTEAU BELLEVUE

SHADED BY LIME TREES, THE SEVENTEENTH-CENTURY CHARTREUSE STILL RESOUNDS WITH THE VOICES OF STONE CARVERS AT WORK.

Bellevue is aptly named. From the middle road, facing Château Angélus, a footpath meanders through a grove of over two hectares of rare tree species: Aleppo pines, arbutus, holm oaks, bay, cedar, olive, osage-orange and even a few wild orchids. The hilltop offers a panoramic view of the region: the steeple of the Saint-Émilion church, the Chapelle Mazerat, the Romanesque church of Saint-Martin and, beyond that, the churches of Libourne and Pomerol. On a clear night, you may even see the lights of Bordeaux.

Shaded by lime trees, the seventeenth-century chartreuse whose terraces are hemmed with antique balusters still resounds with the voices of stone carvers at work. Such was the dream of Maurice de Boüard. Seventy years later, his children and grandchildren, the owners of Château Angélus, made it a reality. In 2007, they purchased the estate, which they shared with the Pradel de Lavaux. The two families joined their efforts to run the property, restructured the vineyard and renovated the vathouse and the magnificent chartreuse, giving it a new future. Now the wines bear the signature of Hubert de Boüard.

CHÂTEAU BERGAT

THE ESTATE IS SHELTERED
BY THE WALLS
AND ANCIENT STONES
OF SAINT-ÉMILION.

Standing on the site since time immemorial, the rock of Bergat gave its name to the château. Next to La Serre, the Bergat vineyard stretches out on the soft-sloping hills at the back of Saint-Émilion, about two hundred yards away from the city walls. They owe to their southern exposition a beneficial day-long dose of sunshine, while the estate is sheltered by the walls and ancient stones of Saint-Émilion. Bergat currently belongs to the Castéja family, who have been running it as tenant farmers since 1952. The same family also owns the Château TrotteVieille, a First Great Classified Growth, in Saint-Émilion. Philippe Castéja runs this ancient four-hectare vineyard that has been a Great Classified Growth since the first 1955 classification.

CHÂTEAU BERLIQUET

Berliquet is among the most ancient names in the Saint-Émilion wine region — it can be found on the Belleyme maps as early as 1768. In addition, the wine was already setting a record in 1784 for its high sales price — 245 *livres*. Thus, it could be one of the oldest registered examples of a wine known by a proprietary name. In 1918, the estate was acquired by Count Louis de Carles, the last descendant of the old Figeac aristocratic lineage and the grandfather of Patrick de Lesquen, the current owner, who lives at the château. The Carles — who are famous in the region through Vital Carles, a canon who founded the Bordeaux hospital in the fourteenth century — acquired many Saint-Émilion wine properties throughout the centuries. Beautifully located on the La Madeleine plateau, over the last few years the vineyard has received a great deal of work and intense care in order to bring out the best of a great wine, aged in centuries-old underground caves.

CHÂTEAU
CADET BON

Bon has been known as the name of a prosperous Saint-Émilion family since the thirteenth century. Several jurats, city judges or mayors, were born into it. In the fourteenth century, Jacques Bon, known as le Cadet (the Younger), planted a vineyard on the hill just north of Saint-Émilion. Since then, the place has been called "La butte du Cadet". The vineyard is still to be found in the same location, right on the city's outskirts, covering seven hectares including six on one undivided plot. The soil — limestone bedrock on a layer of clay — shares its qualities with the soils of the great Saint-Émilion hill, particularly with the presence of asteriated limestone, which is characteristic of the appellation.

Guy and Michèle Richard, both intense wine lovers, bought the property in December 2001 and chose the château's fountain as its graphic symbol. The theme of the Cadet Bon fountain is related to a poem by Homer, in which Dionysus, having been abducted by pirates, pulled out his flute and played. The pirate ship was instantly filled up with wine while the oars and rigging were immobilized by creeping vine branches. Then the pirates were thrown into the sea and turned into dolphins. The fountain is now shown on all the wine labels. The wine estate, which has been through a few hard times, was reborn recently thanks to the renovation of both the buildings and vineyard.

BON HAS BEEN KNOWN AS THE NAME OF A PROSPEROUS SAINT-ÉMILION FAMILY SINCE THE THIRTEENTH CENTURY.

CHÂTEAU
CADET-PIOLA

CADET-PIOLA'S
SEPIA-COLOURED LABEL,
PRINTED WITH
A TIMELESS, BUCOLIC
SCENE

Three hundred meters away from the village, on top of the north hill of Saint-Émilion, the charming Cadet-Piola vineyard could be admired as far back as Roman times. The name Cadet is linked to a former hamlet, while the parallel furrows bordering the vine rows and the five thousand square meters of underground natural caves, hand-carved from the limestone, testify to a long viticultural tradition on the site. Today, the seven hectares of Cadet-Piola, like its illustrious neighbours Château Soutard, Château Larmande and Château Grand Faurie La Rose, are managed by the La Mondiale insurance group.

Cadet-Piola's sepia-coloured label, printed with a timeless, bucolic scene straight from the eighteenth century, makes the wine easy to spot at a glance. Made with passion and a dedication to authenticity, Cadet-Piola may be accurately described as "natural, classic and joyful".

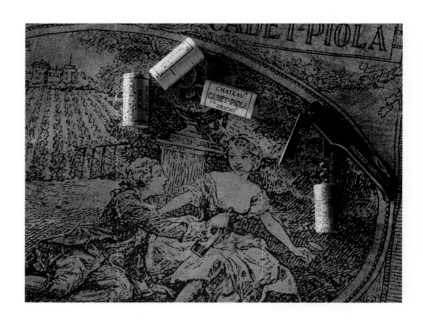

CHÂTEAU
CANON LA GAFFELIÈRE

A NEW PHILOSOPHY
WAS INSTILLED
INTO THE VINEYARD.

In the nineteenth century, the Château Canon La Gaffelière was named La Gaffelière-Boitard after its owner. The present name did not appear until the mid-nineteenth century, though its origin remains unknown aside from La Gaffelière, which is simply the name of the place. In 1971, the estate was bought by Count Hubert Joseph von Neipperg, born into a famous family of German-born landowners. In 1985, his son, Stephan von Neipperg, took over the property and carried out extensive construction work. The château itself — a Girondine that had remained empty for many years — was thoroughly renovated.

At the same time, a winemaking team was formed and a new philosophy was instilled into the vineyard — *Welcome back to the future*, as Stephan von Neipperg would succintly put it. His approach to winemaking is based on respect for nature and tradition, uniting past, present and future; and his aim is to preserve and enhance the potentiality of each terroir, in order to pass on the family heritage to future generations and to assure the wine's durable success. Through his efforts, Canon La Gaffelière has reached the top position among the Great Classified Growths.

CHÂTEAU CAP DE MOURLIN

Cap de Mourlin is the original birthplace of the Capdemourlin family — a rather rare case of a family who still lives on the land to which they owe their name. The Capdemourlins own other châteaux in the Bordeaux region, but this one is their most ancient belonging. With its façade covered in Virginia creeper, the Girondine mansion has the very special charm of a family house. The vineyard, formerly managed in separate lots by brothers Jean and Roger Capdemourlin, then by Mme Capdemourlin and her nephew Jacques, was reunited into a single estate in 1982 — fourteen hectares less than a kilometer away from the village of Saint-Émilion.

Jacques Capdemourlin, now helped by his son Thierry, has managed to bring the wine back to its former glory through every available means, including massive renovation work in the vineyard, in the vathouse and in the barrel cellar, introducing cutting-edge winemaking technology and combining it with traditional barrel ageing before the wine is bottled.

CHÂTEAU
CHAUVIN

IN ANCIENT FRENCH, THE NAME CHAUVIN MEANS "BARE LANDS".

Very close to Pomerol, the Château Chauvin vineyard stretches out over fifteen hectares, all in one piece, facing the Saint-Émilion village. A former smallholding of Cheval Blanc, it fell into the hands of a certain Victor Ondet in 1891. In ancient French, the name Chauvin means "bare lands", actually a perfectly good terroir for vine, which helped the château to obtain the title of Saint-Émilion Great Classified Growth in 1954, in the first edition of the classification.

Now, Victor's great-granddaughters Marie-France and Béatrice, respectively a medical doctor and a chemist, perpetuate the tradition by searching and innovating with passion, striving to bring out the best of the Chauvin vineyard. The landscaped garden, complete with rose bushes and lots of serenity, is a perfect prelude to a visit of this very ladylike wine château.

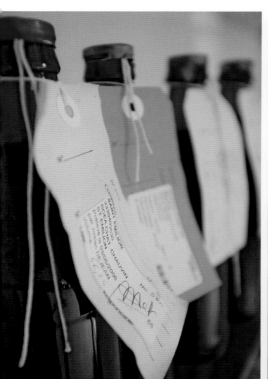

CHÂTEAU CORBIN

❧

THE FOURTH GENERATION OF CORBIN LADIES

The founding of Château Corbin may be dated back to the fifteenth century. Legend has it that Corbin was at the core of a fief belonging to the famous Black Prince, Edward Plantagenet, prince of Wales and Aquitaine. Today, though, the estate is somewhat a ladies' business. Since 1924, the property has remained in the same family and passed on from mother to daughter. Oenologist Anabelle Bardinet-Cruse, the fourth generation of Corbin ladies, and her husband Sébastien have been living at the château with their family for ten years. Her winemaking skills and the particular, dual nature of the terroir, made up of clay and ancient sands, allow Corbin to produce extremely complex wines. Now, they bear her signature. With its eighteenth-century façade and its homogeneous thirteen hectares, bordering the Pomerol appellation, one of the oldest wine châteaux in Saint-Émilion continues to demonstrate, throughout the years, a perfectly elegant, refined style.

CHÂTEAU
CORBIN MICHOTTE

A FIEF THAT BELONGED TO THE BLACK PRINCE, EDWARD PLANTAGENET

Jean-Noël Boidron inherited his passion for wine from his parents and grandparents, who have been making wine since 1855. With such an upbringing, he had no difficulty in acquiring the necessary technical skills, both in winemaking and in oenology, a science that he later taught at the Bordeaux university. He also renovated the house, a nineteenth-century Girondine formerly part of a fief that belonged to the Black Prince, Edward Plantagenet, Prince of Wales and Aquitaine. In 1980, he completely rebuilt the vathouse and cellars to promote a more delicate handling of the grapes and a better respect for their quality. Since then, Jean-Noël and his children have dedicated all their love to this Great Classified Growth of seven hectares in the gravelly zone of Saint-Émilion, bordering the Pomerol appellation.

ALFRESCO LUNCHES
AT CHÂTEAU DASSAULT
HAVE BECOME A MUCH-
AWAITED RENDEZVOUS.

CHÂTEAU
DASSAULT

Château Dassault was born from the willpower of a great engineer — Marcel Dassault, who in 1955 bought the Château Couperie, in Saint-Émilion, "on a perfectly rational impulse", as he liked to say. He renamed it after himself, endowed it with the best technical equipment, and watched the quality of the wine improve year after year. In 1969, Château Dassault became a Great Classified Growth. For that, the work of an excellent team of winemakers deserves to be praised, for, over three generations, they have succeeded in making Dassault one of the best wines of the appellation.

Today, Laurent Dassault watches over the property's reputation. With the help of Laurence Brun, he strives to improve quality on a permanent basis: painstaking work in the vineyard leads to optimal maturity of the grapes; optical sorting for a perfect selection; plot-by-plot winemaking to respect the terroir; ageing in new oak barrels and so on. The barrel cellar was entirely renovated; the bottle cellar has a grey concrete floor and is lit by blue lightbulbs that give it the aspect of landing tracks. And Laurent Dassault likes to welcome the world of wine. In recent years, alfresco lunches at Château Dassault have become a much-awaited rendezvous for his many friends and acquaintances.

CHÂTEAU DESTIEUX

BRINGING
TO LIGHT ALL
THE ASSETS OF
AN EXCEPTIONAL
TERROIR

The name, evolved long ago from the French words *des yeux* ("of the eyes"), hints at the extensive view that can be enjoyed from the château, perched on the topmost heights of the Saint-Émilion region, right next to Laroque. The Destieux vineyard, eight hectares all in one piece, overlooks a magnificent landscape from the Dordogne valley to the Montagne hills. For more than thirty years, Château Destieux has been the property of the Dauriac family, who have succeeded in improving the wine's quality through constant, thorough work at the vineyard and in the cellars, bringing to light all the assets of an exceptional terroir.

Wine is a family tradition for the Dauriacs. The château was bought in 1971 by Mme Dauriac, the current owner's mother. Christian Dauriac, a trained oenologist and medical biologist, has always managed to conciliate his two passions — wine and biology. With the help and sage advice of his friend Michel Rolland, he has constantly developed the family vineyard. The vathouse was entirely restructured and the château was renovated before being decorated with an abundance of antique furniture and paintings, another one of Christian's passions. Finally, the property's classification proved to be the just reward of his painstaking work.

CHÂTEAU
FAURIE DE SOUCHARD

ONE OF THE BEST-EXPOSED LANDS ON THE NORTH SLOPE OF SAINT-ÉMILION

As demonstrated in the pages of a sales register dated 1808, the property was already in existence in the eighteenth century. In 1933, Simone and Maurice Jabiol bought it and gave it its current configuration — a vast, fourteen-hectare rectangle on clay-limestone and clayey sands, one of the best-exposed lands on the north slope of Saint-Émilion. In 2006, Françoise and Alain Sciard, who had followed the Jabiols on the estate in the early 1980s, passed it on to their children, entrusting them with the task of writing a new page of the family property's history.

The Faurie de Souchard team, led by Geoffroy and Thibaud Sciard, now strives to create a great wine from vintage to vintage, achieving perfect quality equally in vine-growing, winemaking and ageing. They should be commended for leading Faurie de Souchard into modern times.

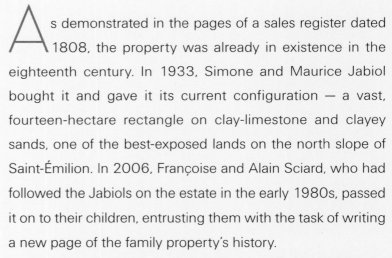

CHÂTEAU
FLEUR CARDINALE

A NEW LIFE OF PASSION, CREATIVITY AND RISK-TAKING

Dominique Decoster — formerly the owner of the luxury Haviland chinaware company in Limoges — and his wife Florence had always liked good wine and nature. Not surprisingly, after they fell in love with the Saint-Émilion region and particularly with Fleur Cardinale, they decided to throw themselves into a new adventure, devoting their entire time and energy to this great château. Located east of Saint-Émilion, on the excellent clay-limestone plateau, Fleur Cardinale has been undergoing a thorough renovation process during the last few years. The red-and-white barrel cellar appears below the château, amid the eighteen hectares of vines, while the house, circled with box hedges, overlooks the vineyard itself as a charming and discreet expression of its owners' refined taste. Dominique and Florence live there on a permanent basis, steadily nurturing a passion for Saint-Émilion, their adopted homeland since the spring of 2001. Ultimately, the classification of Fleur Cardinale was their reward for their choice of a new life of passion, creativity and risk-taking.

CHÂTEAU
FONPLÉGADE

SPECIAL CARE
WAS DEVOTED TO
THE VATHOUSE
AND CELLAR.

Evolved from the Latin "full fountain" or "bent fountain", the name of Château Fonplégade alludes to the springs that run on the upper side of the property. Originally, it was a set of vine plots belonging to several different owners. In 1852, Jean-Pierre Beylot purchased Fonplégade, building the château and the winemaking buildings. Through purchases and inheritances, year after year, the estate acquired its present shape: eighteen hectares all in one block. In 2004, it was bought by Stephen Adams, a wine-loving American businessman who set out to write a new page on the château's history book with the aim of opening the place to the public.

The old walls have been preserved, but there is considerable change inside. Special care was devoted to the vathouse and cellar. Above all, Stephen Adams, taught by the experience of owning wineries in the United States, wishes to open the entire château to visitors, from the shop to the tasting room. Even the private sections have been redesigned

for greeting guests — his wife, Denise Adams, has personally supervised the design work on interior decoration. The reception room, lit by a gigantic chandelier and set around a huge table, seems to be the place where everything converges, while the bedrooms and apartments, complete with toile de Jouy and antique furniture, have a soft and refined atmosphere. A perfect harmony for this neoclassical yet very contemporary château.

CHÂTEAU
FONROQUE

THE RESULT OF DEEP
CONTEMPLATION,
A CAREFUL SENSE
OF PLANNING
AND A RESPECTFUL,
PHILOSOPHICAL CON-
NECTION TO THE EARTH.

The original birthplace of the Moueix family stands at the end of an alley of hornbeam trees. The place is brimming with stories, anecdotes and memories confirming their ancestral love for this piece of land, now managed by Alain Moueix. In 1931, his great-grandparents settled on the estate; this was the start of a long, fascinating adventure, of which Alain is currently writing a brand-new chapter while striving to harmonize past and future. Since 2003, he has been directing his efforts towards organic vine-growing — the result of deep contemplation, a careful sense of planning and a respectful, philosophical connection to the earth. Gradually, the use of biodynamics has been extended to the entire vineyard — about eighteen hectares — to make the environmental experience worthwhile. Winemaking at Fonroque is the result of painstaking research and experimentation leading to harmony, balance and the expression of a fully alive terroir, uniting with the winemaker and his vision to make a coherent entity.

CHÂTEAU
FRANC MAYNE

WHERE ECCENTRIC CHIC MEETS CONTEMPORARY DESIGN

Flanking the Côte de Franc and bordering the ancient Roman road, Franc-Mayne's seven hectares are laid out around a sixteenth-century post inn leading into ancient stone quarries, among the most extensive in Saint-Émilion since they cover more than two hectares — a historical landmark also used for the ageing of wine in barrels. An impressive visit indeed! Griet Van Malderen-Laviale and her husband Hervé Laviale bought the property at the beginning of 2005. They converted the old Girondine mansion into a nine-bedroom boutique hotel — nine quirky, highly personalized rooms, with names such as Indian Fusion, British Landscape or African Lodge like so many invitations to travel where eccentric chic meets contemporary design. A tasteful decor of antique furniture, splendid silks and the house's original mantelpieces. Under the dining room's huge baroque chandelier, both hosts and guests enjoy a delicious traditional cuisine washed down with the château's wines, either the grand vin or its younger brother, Les Cèdres de Franc Mayne. An allusion to the cedar trees spreading their branches above a natural garden complete with water plants and a swimming pool filled with natural running water.

AT THE HEART OF
THIS GREAT ESTATE

CHÂTEAU
GRAND CORBIN

All the Corbin estates can be traced back to a now disappeared, much larger domain that belonged to the Prince of Wales, the eldest son of King Edward III of England, better known as the Black Prince because of the burnished sheen of his steel armour. The Grand Corbin vineyard is no exception and was right at the heart of this great estate. In medieval times, two important seigneuries, Figeac and Corbin, shared the Saint-Émilion territory. Their name is still attached to a large number of remaining properties, the Corbin estates having been most probably created in 1852, when the land was divided up.

Savinien Giraud, also the owner of Château Trotanoy in Pomerol, presided over the winemakers' union of Saint-Émilion, while his cousin Joseph traded wines in Libourne. In 1924, Joseph, on Savinien's advice, decided to purchase Château Corbin and settled there with his wife and three children. In 1936, bad sales in the wine trade led his second son, Alain, into seeking employment in northern France. Although he stayed there until 1973, in 1960 he had the opportunity to acquire Château Grand Corbin, next to his parents' vineyard, and ran it until his death in 1982. Today, his eldest son, Philippe, is at the head of this fifteen-hectare wine estate.

CHÂTEAU
GRAND CORBIN-DESPAGNE

THE AWARDING OF
SEVERAL MEDALS
CONFIRMED ITS
REPUTATION

Grand Corbin-Despagne is located north of Saint-Émilion, in the heart of a former Pomerol that which used to belong to the Black Prince, Edward Plantagenet. The place itself, called Grand Corbin, lends its name to the label Château Grand Corbin-Despagne, created in 1812. The name also shows an association with the Despagne family, a familiar name in the history of Saint-Émilion for more than four centuries. The oldest document mentioning their existence is the birth certificate, dated 1665, of ploughman Pierre Despagne's first child. Their descendant Louis, born in 1789, played an important role in the family's expansion. In 1812, he settled at the place called Corbin, not far from Cheval Blanc where his grandfather on his mother's side lived as a tenant farmer. Until he died in 1845, his only concern was to build up a sizeable vineyard. In 1852, his son Jean, purchasing twenty hectares of neighboring land, gave the property the structure it has retained almost a century and a half later. In the early twentieth century, soon after Grand Corbin-Despagne became an authentic wine entity, the awarding of several medals confirmed its reputation.

Today, the seventh generation of Despagnes is at work on the vineyard. With much passion, enthusiasm and respect, François runs the property where he has recently decided to live with his family. After 1996, he decided to introduce integrated pest control into his vineyard, following every rule of the Terra Vitis charter for sustainable growing. Today, he devotes himself to the terroir and to the vine plant, to which he applies the principles of organic winemaking. With one single purpose in mind: his land, his grapes, his family.

CHÂTEAU
GRAND MAYNE

FROM THE PORCH,
THE VIEW OVER
THE VINEYARDS AT SUNSET
IS MAGNIFICENT.

The name Mayne is derived from the word *manoir*, meaning manor, and originally "a beautiful mansion surrounded by a sizeable surface of land". The estate lies for the most part on clay-limestone and limestone plateaux. The impressive and homogeneous architectural ensemble was built during the sixteenth and the seventeenth centuries in stone from the underground Saint-Émilion limestone quarries. The château and its square courtyard, oriented north and south at the foot of the hill, overlook the plain and the surrounding vineyards. The park in which they stand is enclosed by rough-stone and freestone walls over two feet thick.

The architects of the time intended to protect the château both from intruders and from ocean winds; to achieve that, they built a structure sixty meters long, facing full west, whose façade is harmoniously parted in the middle by a semicircular arched porch through which horse carriages used to enter the château. From the porch, the view over the vineyards at sunset is magnificent. Discovering the château — a long stone

ship resting on a sea of vines — is equally ravishing. Inside, the original oak timber framework adds to the beauty of the place. The vineyard currently covers seventeen hectares, all Great Classified Growth — the heart of the original estate. Jean Nony, a wine trader from Corrèze who resided in the Bordeaux business district of Les Chartrons, bought Grand Mayne in 1934, while the great economic crisis of 1929 was still making itself felt. After him, from 1977 to 2001, his son Jean-Pierre took charge of the management. Since the death of her husband Jean-Pierre, Marie-Françoise Nony, with the help of her sons Jean-Antoine and Damien, has been maintaining the tradition.

CHÂTEAU GRAND PONTET

❧

BRINGING OUT THE CHARM AND FEMININE GRACE OF THIS *GRAND CRU.*

Standing only seven hundred meters from the Saint-Émilion collegiate church, Château Grand Pontet is also neighbour to First Classified Great Growth Château Beau-Séjour Bécot. Like her brothers, Sylvie Pourquet Bécot has been running this large family estate of fourteen hectares on the west plateau, all in one piece, for ten years. Constant investment for a quarter of a century, extreme care and attention devoted to winemaking and ageing, and a great respect for the terroir have led the team to full success in bringing out the charm and feminine grace of this *grand cru.*

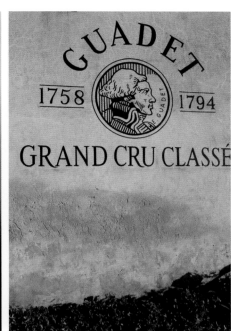

CHÂTEAU
GUADET

Château Guadet has the peculiarity of being nestled in the very heart of the Saint-Émilion village, on the top of the high limestone plateau. It was named after the Girondist deputy Marguerite Élie Guadet, who became famous during the French Revolution. He was said to have hidden with his companions in the magnificent caves that run underneath the property — now located at number 4, rue Guadet. The main street of Saint-Émilion bears his name, and his profile is printed on the wine's label, perpetuating his memory. Five successive generations on the estate are an asset for Guy Petrus Lignac, helping this nature-loving man to put in practice, both in the vineyard and in the cellar, a seamless philosophy based on respect for the vine plant and its fruit. With the help of oenologist Stéphane Derenoncourt, he wields the tools of modern technology and traditional skills.

IN THE VERY HEART OF THE SAINT-ÉMILION VILLAGE

CHÂTEAU
HAUT-CORBIN

THE HISTORY MAY BE SOBER, BUT THE LAND IS NOT.

Haut-Corbin may be counted among the châteaux that wrote the history of the Saint-Émilion region. Back when the English were "reaping" Aquitaine, Haut-Corbin, as all the other Corbin estates, was part of a vast fief belonging to Edward, Prince of Wales, also known as the Black Prince, the son of Edward III. As decades went by, the land was partitioned, giving birth to a variety of wine estates on the north side of the appellation, all named after Corbin. In spite of this illustrious past, Haut-Corbin's history is rather quiet, the name appearing scarcely in the local sources. The history may be sober, but the land is not. Half a mile away from the greatest vineyards of Pomerol, Haut-Corbin's terroir has a lot to say for itself, producing wines in which the best of both origins is combined.

When the Mutuelles d'Assurances du Bâtiment et des Travaux Publics — an insurance company for the building industry — purchased the vineyard in 1986, they wanted this promising estate to recover its former grandeur. In a landscape that takes on the airs of a lovely countryside scene, the renovation work done on the vineyard and on the buildings has revealed, on a soft-sloping hill, a stone house nestled in vine rows and shaded with cypress trees.

CHÂTEAU HAUT-SARPE

THE OWNER HAS TURNED
HIS CELLARS INTO
MUSEUMS DEDICATED
TO THE GLORY OF
GREAT WINES.

The Château Haut-Sarpe, which was awarded a gold medal at the 1867 Paris World Fair, is still quite worthy of the efforts and achievements of Baron Henri du Foussat, who owned it at the time. Encouraged by his success, he had planned to renovate the château and to redesign the park soon after purchasing them. In 1929, Joseph Janoueix, from Corrèze, bought them back. The château is handsome with its Trianon-inspired central aisle and French-style classic gardens. At the time, Saint-Émilion wines were undergoing a period of growth of which Janoueix took advantage, creating his own trading house, renovating the estate and increasing the surface of his vineyard. Two years later, Joseph Janoueix married Marie-Antoinette Estrade, a woman of heart and mind, also a woman of action. Later, their son Jean-François took charge of the family business after his father retired. Remaining true to tradition, he continued to offer lodging to pilgrims on their way to Santiago de Compostela, renovating his other buildings all the while. Hospitality is a serious affair at Haut-Sarpe and the grape harvest is a great moment in the life of the property; the walls resound with the sound of corks being pulled and wine pouring out of the bottles during the many celebrations that are held throughout the year. The owner, who is also a passionate collector, has turned his cellars into museums dedicated to the glory of great wines, age-old winemaking traditions and related trades. His collections of vintage cars and wine-related items may also be seen there.

CHÂTEAU L'ARROSÉE

L'ARROSÉE OWES ITS NAME TO THE PRESENCE OF AN UNDERGROUND SPRING.

Historically, the Château L'Arrosée (*arrosée* meaning "doused") owes its name to the presence of an underground spring. Listed as one of the Saint-Émilion first growths in successive editions of Édouard Féret's *Bordeaux and its Wines: Classified in Order of Merit* as early as 1868, L'Arrosée at the time belonged to Pierre Magne, a member of Emperor Napoléon III's government. Later, it was inherited by the Marquis de Reverseaux de Rouvray, a French ambassador to the court of Vienna. 2002 was the year when Roger Caille, founder of the Jet Services company, and his son Jean-Philippe — both lovers of great Bordeaux wines — threw themselves into the adventure and acquired the nine-and-a-half-hectare vineyard. A decisive date in the history of the château, with the addition of a whole set of technical facilities such as brand-new vathouse and cellars and a cutting-edge sorting table, specially patented by L'Arrosée. As a symbol of L'Arrosée's regeneration, the god Bacchus is displayed both on the walls of the château and on the wine label. Under the impulse of Roger and Jean-Philippe Caille, praised by both amateurs and professionals, the château is now in perfect condition to reach its full potential.

CHÂTEAU LA CLOTTE

DEEP AND FRUITY WINES FROM THEIR MAGNIFICENT TERROIR

One of the oldest and most interesting wine châteaux in the appellation leans against the old city walls, within the city limits of Saint-Émilion: Château La Clotte has been the property of the De Grailly family since the fourteenth century. Originally planted in vines on a surface of twenty hectares, the domain was partitioned over the centuries. The Chailleau family, in 1913, acquired its last plot.

During the years that followed World War II, Georges Chailleau, Grand Vinetier of the Jurade and the proud owner of the Les Logis de la Cadenne restaurant, has elevated this four-hectare vineyard to the highest level of quality. Now, his descendants — the three cousins Nelly, Dominique and Odile — are joining their efforts to extract lively, deep and fruity wines from their magnificent terroir, using modern techniques but with a respect for tradition. La Clotte, which sits upon the underground Saint-Émilion caves where the wines quietly mature, exhales an unmistakable charm. It is a place to enjoy simple family life; warm and friendly tastings are also held on the terrace, which offers one of the most exceptional views over Saint-Émilion.

CHÂTEAU
LA COUSPAUDE

IN MEDIEVAL TIMES, LA COUSPAUDE WAS CALLED "LA CROIX PAUTE".

A symbol of elegance and the very emblem of the château, a huge bronze horse stands in the middle of the eighteenth-century chartreuse's cobbled courtyard, less than five yards away from the Grandes Murailles. One century — that is how long La Couspaude has remained faultlessly true to the descendants of Prosper Jean Robin, who, in 1908, bought this seven-hectare vineyard situated right on the road to Compostelle, the monolithic church of Saint-Émilion being an important stop on the pilgrims' journey. In medieval times, La Couspaude was called "La Croix Paute", a name that referred to a stone cross standing near the entrance to the château.

Four generations later, the Aubert family made La Couspaude the flagship of the Aubert wine company. Today, the story goes on with Vanessa, Héloïse and Yohan, now the masters of the family vineyard. It is now the childrens' responsibility to walk in their elders' tracks and bring out the best of this exceptional heritage.

CHÂTEAU
LA DOMINIQUE

A RICH MERCHANT
WHO HAD RUN
A SUCCESSFUL
BUSINESS ON
THE ISLAND
OF DOMINICA

In the seventeenth and eighteenth centuries, the West Indian trade elevated Bordeaux to the rank of first harbour in the kingdom. The property got its name from its first owner, a rich merchant who had run a successful business on the island of Dominica (*Dominique* in French) and wished to evoke that happy period of his life when he bought the estate in the late eighteenth century. Château La Dominique was already mentioned in the very first issues of *Bordeaux et ses vins*, published by Féret.

In 1969, M. Clément Fayat, a Bordeaux building contractor and a lover of fine wines, bought the property. La Dominique shares nearly one kilometer of its border with Château Cheval Blanc and has other prestigious neighbours, such as La Conseillante and L'Evangile in Pomerol. For Clément Fayat's innovative mind, terroir is nothing if the hand of man does not help its full nature to be expressed. He agrees that every wine produced on his vineyards should be of a flawless quality, but it should also express its own identity and personality. He remains convinced that a great wine is the joint product of nature's work and man's work. That is why he devoted equal care to the thorough renovation of the vineyard and cellars and to the reception and tasting rooms, restoring the property's noble status to its full glory.

CHÂTEAU
LA MARZELLE

THEIR MAIN CONCERN HAS
BEEN TO CONSTITUTE
A NEW TEAM, RENOVATE
THE VINEYARD AND
BUILDINGS, AND RESTORE
LA MARZELLE TO
ITS FORMER GLORY.

On the road to Saint-Émilion, around the Château Grand Barrail hotel, La Marzelle stretches out its thirteen hectares of vineyard on a gravelly, sandy and clayey soil. The property, whose name appeared on the Belleyme map in 1821, was already listed in the first 1955 classification. It owes its name to Édouard de La Marzelle, a late-nineteenth-century politician.

In 1998, Jean-Jacques and Jacqueline Sioen, two Belgian textile manufacturers and the creators of Sioen Industries, bought the château. Since their arrival, their main concern has been to constitute a new team, renovate the vineyard and buildings, and restore La Marzelle to its former glory. Gradually, the château is starting a new life, welcoming contemporary artists and designers and displaying their production, for the Sioens are also a family of art lovers. Meanwhile, a new life is also breathed into the soil, the vegetative cycle of the vine is studied with great attention and everything is done by the current winemaking team to respect the identity of this terroir.

CHÂTEAU
LA SERRE

Two hundred meters away from the city walls, La Serre enjoys an exceptional view over its prestigious neighbours: Pavie Macquin, whose magnificent oak trees may be seen in the distance; Troplong Mondot and TrotteVieille; and, further east, Ausone and La Tour du Roy. According to legend, the property could owe its name to its ideal full south orientation (la serre meaning "greenhouse"). The classic seventeenth-century house was built by Romain de Labayme, born into a very old local family which produced jurats, attorneys at the Bordeaux Parliament and even five mayors between 1541 and 1728, the last of them being called "Sieur de Lassère".

Bought in the 1950s by the family of the current owner Luc d'Arfeuillle, La Serre and its park are set into a seven-hectare vineyard on the limestone Saint-Émilion plateau, sitting on top of a network of underground caves on two or three levels. The house itself has no underground cellar, for at the time when it was built quarrymen did not dig under houses. Behind the ivy-clad walls, a treasure of history and memory is kept by the friendly hosts.

ACCORDING TO LEGEND, THE PROPERTY COULD OWE ITS NAME TO ITS IDEAL FULL SOUTH ORIENTATION.

CHÂTEAU
LA TOUR DU PIN

IT IS NOW AT THE BEGINNING OF A NEW LIFE.

The two La Tour du Pin wine estates used to be one large domain that belonged to the De La Tour Figeac family. This one was detached from the larger Figeac estate in 1879, before being split in 1902 between two sisters, each one retaining the rights to use the same name for both properties. The La Tour du Pin lot was bought back in 1947 by Jean-Michel Moueix. The tower that gave its name to the château still stands there, but it is now looking towards Cheval Blanc, to which it has belonged since 2006. Standing close to the famous vineyard, it is now at the beginning of a new life.

CHÂTEAU LA TOUR DU PIN FIGEAC

La Tour du Pin Figeac and La Tour du Pin shared the same history until July 15, 1902, when the land was divided as the result of inheritance rights. The vineyard was originally part of the larger Figeac estate, from which it was dissociated in 1879. Two sisters inherited the two properties, both of which held on to the same name for many years. In 1981, the names of owners Giraud and Bellivier were added to La Tour du Pin in order to distinguish the two châteaux, standing side by side, between Figeac and Cheval Blanc.

With both their names added to the château's name, the owners were perpetuating an ancient tradition. In an equally traditional manner, the Girauds, who currently live on the estate, like to welcome groups of harvesters at vendanges time, seating them around large tables where cheerful dinners are held, with the added joy of returning each year.

CHÂTEAU
LA TOUR FIGEAC

Château La Tour Figeac owes its name to a tower that still stood on the property at the end of the eighteenth century. La Tour Figeac was originally part of the larger Figeac estate, from which it was separated in 1882. At that time, the property covered about forty hectares. It was later divided in two parts — La Tour Figeac and the surface now covered by the two La Tour du Pin Figeac. Still later, the property was handed down to the Rapin family, who built the Directoire-style chartreuse in 1958. In 1973, the German-born Rettenmaier family bought the property, which has been run since 1994 by Otto Maximilian Rettenmaier, who generously welcomes his friends and clients from all over the world. An accomplished music lover with a special fondness for classical music, Otto named each one of his fermenting vats after some famous composer — Mozart, Tchaikovsky, Purcell, Beethoven, Vivaldi, Dvorak… while the ladies who work in the cellars chose to name the keeping tanks after international female jazz singers and musicians — Ella, Dee Dee, Rhoda, Liza…

CHÂTEAU
LANIOTE

THE PROPERTY
WAS PASSED ON
FROM MOTHER
TO DAUGHTER FOR
SEVEN GENERATIONS.

Château Laniote has been in the hands of the same family for about two centuries. In 1816, wine trader Pierre Lacoste bought a cellar and a few vine stocks around it, adding a few plots here and there until 1844. He also owned some of the city's catacombs, the thirteenth-century Chapelle de la Trinité and the hermitage that sheltered the monk Émilion. The Laniote vineyard, joined together from different plots in the mid-nineteenth century, has not been modified since, while the property was passed on from mother to daughter for seven generations until Madame de La Filolie.

Since 1989, Arnaud de La Filolie, with the help of his wife Florence Ribéreau Gayon — herself from a famous family of Bordeaux oenologists — has run this family property with great enthusiasm, together striving to respect the Saint-Émilion traditions while applying innovative methods and the latest scientific knowledge to their winemaking. They also like to welcome many visitors throughout the year, sharing their passion for their wine and terroir.

CHÂTEAU
LARCIS DUCASSE

THE HOUSE HAS
THE CHARM OF AN
OLD FAMILY HOME.

In the eighteenth century, a Bordeaux family named Raba prospered as a result of maritime commerce, at the time a flourishing activity. A century later, in 1893, Henri Raba, a lover of great wines, purchased the Château Larcis Ducasse and enthusiastically invested a large part of his own fortune in the vineyard, building one of the first gravitational vathouses in the region, supported by iron columns reputedly designed by Gustave Eiffel. After his death, in 1925, his wife and his son André took over the estate. André died during World War II without descendants, so his niece Hélène Gratiot Alphandéry inherited the property in 1941. Herself in danger, she escaped to the unoccupied zone of France with her two children before coming back to take care of the property after the Liberation. Her son, Jacques Olivier Gratiot, took over in 1990. Under his influence, the long tradition of quality for which Larcis Ducasse is known was maintained and improved.

For the last few years, following the advice of manager Nicolas Thienpont, the owners have adopted environmentally friendly growing methods, joining him in his efforts to improve quality. The vineyard enjoys an exceptional "Mediterranean" orientation to the full south on terraced plots. The house, graced with an enclosed garden and a square-shaped stone well in the middle of the courtyard, has the charm of an old family home — a charm that Olivier Gratiot and Jeanne Attmane, his sister, maintain with much affection.

CHÂTEAU
LARMANDE

IT IS SAID THAT
CERTAIN FAMOUS
JURATS USED TO HOLD
THEIR MEETINGS THERE.

Château Larmande, which is mentioned in the Saint-Émilion archives as early as 1585, is one of the oldest wine estates in the appellation. It is said that certain famous jurats used to hold their meetings there. In the early twentieth century, the property was offered as a wedding gift to Alice Capdemourlin and Fernand Méneret. Three generations of Ménerets lived and worked on this vineyard, a little less than a mile away from the old village. In the late 1990s, Jean Méneret, a famous figure in the world of Bordeaux wines who elevated the property to the highest quality level, sold the Château Larmande to the La Mondiale insurance company. Today, the property is run by Claire Thomas-Chenard, a graduate of the Bordeaux oenology faculty, as are all the other vineyards belonging to the AG2R-La Mondiale insurance group — Château Soutard, Château Cadet-Piola, and Château Grand Faurie La Rose. Provided with state-of-the-art technical equipment in 2003, the twenty-two hectares

of Château Larmande now enjoy international fame while remaining true to their owner's respect for tradition. The harvest testifies to it: Every year, the same teams of forty grape harvesters are happy to meet again around the long picnic tables. And the famous pink Larmande bottle cap is the unmistakable proof of a feminine touch.

CHÂTEAU
LAROQUE

At the end of a long alley of cedar trees, the famous, intricately ornate wrought-iron gate of Laroque — actually the former choir gate from the Soissons cathedral — opens out onto one of the most impressive wine châteaux in the region. Since the earliest times, Laroque has dominated the Saint-Émilion vineyard. Its origins may be traced back to the Anglo-Norman invasions. Its setting, on a rocky hilltop, reveals its former defensive role: protecting the city and its surroundings from attacks of various enemies. From this medieval past remain a massive twelfth-century tower and the moat, which was kept intact in the eighteenth century, when the château was rebuilt in the new style with an abundance of French windows opening out onto the gardens, the courtyards and the countryside. The Beaumartins bought the estate in 1935. In 1982, the owners and their team set themselves an ambitious challenge, no less than a quest for excellence. The vineyard was extended to sixty-one hectares. Since 2004, Xavier Beaumartin has been running the estate, putting into practice the family's deep affection and concern for this vineyard. Now, Château Laroque has recovered its splendour. A "Klein blue" vathouse, a contemporary tasting room, may be admired for its decor, based on classic paintings and antique furniture of the vast château rooms.

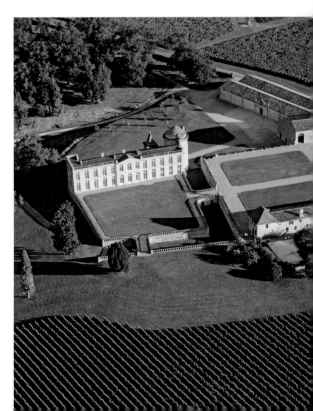

CHÂTEAU
LAROZE

"LAROZE WAS CREATED BY A WOMAN — MY GREAT-GRANDMOTHER — IN 1882".

"Laroze was created by a woman — my great-grand-mother — in 1882, and was passed on to me by my grandmother during the 1960s," says Guy Meslin, the current manager of the property, hinting at the family history. Indeed, only a woman could have given a flower name to this estate, maybe as a reminder of the rose bushes planted at the end of vine rows, but more certainly as a symbol of the wine's fragrance, which is sure to raise enthusiasm in every taster. The Meslins are directly descended from the estate's founders, the Gurchy family, and are from a long lineage of winemakers. They were already mentioned as producers in Saint-Émilion, in a place called Mazerat, as early as 1610. Two centuries later, they joined three small estates together to obtain a twenty-seven-hectare vineyard. Two years after that, in 1885, they built the château in late-nineteenth-century Beaux Arts style, before laying plans for the vathouse and cellar.

Nestled at the foot of the northwest hill of Saint-Émilion, the vineyard seems to roll up around the château. The 1955 classification rewarded the founders' efforts and the hard work of those who followed them on the property. In 1990, Guy Meslin inherited the estate from his father, restructuring the vineyard, the buildings and the technical equipment. The style and quality improved; the wines of Laroze were taken to an unprecedented level of richness, elegance and fruitiness — a result of the expert, thorough work done by the winemaking team in recent decades.

CHÂTEAU
LE PRIEURÉ

❧

"BELIEVING IN THE EARTH; SHOWING RESPECT FOR ITS FUTURE"

Château Le Prieuré and the history of the Brisson-Guichard family are closely intertwined. From 1832 to 1949, the Brisson-Guichards purchased several estates: Siaurac in Lalande de Pomerol; Vray Croix de Gay in Pomerol, and Le Prieuré. In each generation, members of the family played a substantial part in the political and social affairs of the region. In 1998, encouraged by his daughter Aline and Paul Goldschmidt, his son-in-law, former state minister and famous Gaullist from the Fifth French Republic, Olivier Guichard decided to upgrade the property. When he died, in 2004, Aline and her husband abandoned Paris and their own jobs to take their share of the tradition. They restructured the château and vineyard with the intention of opening them to the public and to professionals.

The small cellar was renovated and modernized; a huge wooden terrace was built so that the magnificent view over the Saint-Émilion valley could be enjoyed. The six hectares of Le Prieuré, nestled among the finest terroirs on the high Saint-Émilion plateau, facing TrotteVieille and bordering Troplong-Mondot and Pavie-Macquin, were made a Great Classified Growth as early as 1955. "Believing in the earth; showing respect for its future" with elegance and finesse — a philosophy Aline and Paul passionately uphold, as a tribute to Madeleine Brisson, a young lady who, in 1918, through her engagement to Baron Louis Guichard, brought the vineyards of her gentle native Gironde into her husband's family.

"Croire à la terre, respecter son futur."

CHÂTEAU
LES GRANDES
MURAILLES

A symbolic image of Saint-Émilion, Les Grandes Murailles is named after a famous wall that survives from the Dominican monastery, which used to stand on the outskirts of Saint-Émilion in the twelfth century and was torn down during the French Wars of Religion. With a surface of two hectares on a clay-limestone plateau, quite close to the centre of the village, this is — by size — one of the smallest Classified Growths in Saint-Émilion.

The cellar, which was hidden inside the stone quarries in 1996, cannot be seen from the road. With a huge wrought-iron gate leading into it, it is a true underground labyrinth in the deepest heart of Saint-Émilion, where the very layers of that fabulous terroir and even the roots of the vines planted above are visible. Unusually, the cellar houses both the vathouse and the rows of new oak barrels where the wines are aged. Sophie Fourcade Reiffers, a descendant of a family who settled in Saint-Émilion in 1643, looks after the property, where the most precious antique artefacts have been affectionately preserved: the sculptures from the Croix Saint-Jacques and a sculpted acanthus leaf that used to adorn the foot of a Gothic ogive.

CLOSE TO THE CENTRE OF THE VILLAGE, THIS IS — BY SIZE — ONE OF THE SMALLEST CLASSIFIED GROWTHS.

CHÂTEAU
MATRAS

THE VINEYARD CERTAINLY HAS A LONG HISTORY.

The vathouse and cellar of this family-owned Great Classified Growth are installed in the Mazerat chapel, built in the twelfth century in the southwestern part of the village — a way of placing oneself under the protection of the authorities who developed and maintained winemaking in the region. A matras was originally a crossbow quarrel with a small bulging end; in medieval times, the meaning was extended to the man who carried the weapon. It is therefore possible that the place owes its name to a soldier who, during the Hundred Years' War, settled there when trouble receded. And it is just as possible that the same soldier planted some vines on the land.

Whatever the truth, the vineyard certainly has a long history — it is mentioned on one of the oldest maps of the region, drawn around 1763 by Belleyme. Jean Bernard-Lefebvre, who bought the property in 1962, undertook some serious renovation work, particularly in the vineyard — new plantings, and drainage for every plot. Since 1976, the estate has been managed by Véronique Gaboriaud-Bernard, who is equally expert at making and selling the wine.

CHÂTEAU
MONBOUSQUET

When Gérard Perse purchased Château Monbousquet in 1993, a new page in the history of this wine château was turned. Located some five hundred yards from the south hill of Saint-Émilion, Monbousquet, in the course of a few years and under the supervision of its new owner — who also bought the Château Pavie (First Great Classified Growth) and the Château Pavie Decesse (Great Classified Growth) — made its way into the classification and took its place among the greats. This growth, whose origins probably date back to 1540, has been through various stages during its history, and did not recover the status it enjoyed in the nineteenth century until the end of World War II.

However, the most substantial change happened in 1993. As soon as he set foot on the estate, Gérard Perse redefined

the production data, from the thirty-two-hectare vineyard to the buildings. The old vathouse was demolished and built anew, while a barrel cellar was built from scratch. The eighteenth-century château and the seven-hectare wooded park, planted with magnolia and cedar trees, were thoroughly renovated. Utterly seduced by the place and particularly by the vineyard overlooking the valley, Gérard Perse and his wife Chantal settled there. A new adventure began for these passionate entrepreneurs in search of perfection. Guests and friends from all over the world are welcome at the château. And — a rare fact that should be mentioned — Monbousquet is also available in white!

CHÂTEAU
MOULIN DU CADET

Situated on the outskirts of Saint-Émilion, on a limestone plateau named Le Cadet, this charming vineyard has been run since 2002 by Isabelle and Pierre Blois-Moueix. The old château, with an eighteenth-century dovecote on either side, has known some happy times as is shown by the still lively colours of the wall paintings inside the house. And indeed, the wine was awarded a gold medal at the 1867 Paris World Fair.

Before embarking on the renovation the building, the new owners devoted their attention to the wine. A pretty vathouse, overlooking the vineyard, was built in 1991 using traditional building techniques. In 1996, they decided to apply organic growing methods, not only to protect the vineyard but also to help it to express its mineral qualities in the best possible way. Biodynamic culture was first tested on a few plots before being extended to the whole vineyard after 2005. Alain Moueix, Isabelle's brother, is dedicating his international experience and professional rigour to this wonderful terroir, enabling it to be appreciated in all its beauty — the silky delicacy of limestone, the subtle power of clay.

BEFORE EMBARKING
ON THE RENOVATION
OF THE BUILDING,
THE NEW OWNERS DEVOTED
THEIR ATTENTION TO
THE WINE.

THE HISTORY OF CHÂTEAU
PAVIE DECESSE IS CLOSELY
RELATED TO THAT
OF CHÂTEAU PAVIE.

CHÂTEAU
PAVIE DECESSE

The history of Château Pavie Decesse is closely related to that of Château Pavie, which it dominates with all its height, being situated immediately above it. The whole estate, originally dating back to the fourth century, was part of Pavie until the late nineteenth century, when its owner decided to gather a few plots into one independant vineyard that he named Pavie Decesse.

At the time of the 1954 classification, when the château was awarded the status of Great Classified Growth, it belonged to a certain M. Marzelle. When M. Marzelle died, in 1990, Jean-Paul Valette, the owner of Pavie, took charge of the vineyard, which he bought the very same year. Later, in 1997, Gérard Perse, also the owner of Château Monbousquet, purchased both estates — Pavie (First Great Classified Growth) and Pavie Decesse. He did to Pavie Decesse what he did to Monbousquet: A demanding owner, in search of perfection, he led the renovation of the vineyard and buildings in order to obtain the best possible wine. The château now houses the fermenting rooms, and the barrel cellar has been restored to its original architectural style. Pavie Decesse, treated with the same care that was devoted to its elder, now also enjoys the very same assets.

CHÂTEAU
PETIT FAURIE DE SOUTARD

The story begins with a wedding. Françoise, when she married Jacques Capdemourlin, brought to her in-laws — who already owned Château Balestard La Tonnelle and Château Cap de Mourlin — a third jewel to decorate their crown: Petit Faurie de Soutard. Underneath its French-style slate roof, and surrounded by terraced gardens, this is a perfectly lovely nineteenth-century chartreuse. The château stands in the middle of eight hectares of vineyard, on the Saint-Émilion plateau, six hundred meters from the village. Françoise Capdemourlin's favourite values — elegance and femininity — are perfectly expressed by the place. For the last few years, heavy renovation work has also been carried out on the château, in the barrel cellar and in the vathouse to maintain the wine's excellent fame.

CHÂTEAU RIPEAU

⌇

PAINTED CEILINGS IN THE SEVENTEENTH-CENTURY BUCOLIC STYLE, CLASSIC PAINTINGS AND PORTRAITS OF LADIES

Towards the end of the eighteenth century, Château Ripeau belonged to Guillaume Ignace de Bouchereau, *trésorier de France* and one of the most prominent landowners of his time. Later, it fell into the hands of two brothers, Denis and Eugène Buhler, two famous landscape gardeners who designed many French-style parks and gardens. Ripeau's park is no exception, and more than a hundred years later its initial structure is still visible.

In 1917, Ripeau was purchased by the De Wilde family. Later, Marcel Loubat, a wine trader and mayor of Libourne, acquired it and renovated it before giving it over to Suzanne de Wilde, his granddaughter, in 1943. Suzanne's husband, Michel, gave a new energy to the château, which elevated it to the status of Grand Cru Classé as early as 1955, the very first year of the classification. In 1976, they passed the property on to their two children, Jean and Françoise de Wilde. Françoise, who was born at the château, took over and ran the vineyard according to tradition while using state-of-the-art winemaking technology, building a brand new vathouse in 1997.

In 2004, a new generation took control. Barbara Janoueix Coutel, Françoise's daughter, now keeps an eye on the château's management. She lives there with her family, as her mother and grandmother did, in a house that bears the mark of several generations' decorative taste: Bacchic mascarons outside, scenes of bacchanalia inside, painted ceilings in the seventeenth-century bucolic style, classic paintings and portraits of ladies in the rooms — a poetic hint of the owner's love of art and wine.

CHÂTEAU
SAINT-GEORGES CÔTE PAVIE

AN ANCIENT ROMAN
MANSION ONCE STOOD
IN THIS LOCATION.

Judging by the many archaeological remains found in the ground around the property, including some mosaics from the third or fourth century, quite close to a place named Le Palat, it seems clear that an ancient Roman mansion once stood in this location, surrounded by extensive farmland. Could it be the villa of the ancient poet Ausonius, who had been a winemaker before becoming the second most important person in the Roman Empire? No one knows, but the place is certainly perfect for vine-growing, owing to its excellent soil and orientation. Since 1873, this sloping vineyard of five and a half hectares has been the property of one family of wine traders. Four generations followed there with equal success.

Located on the clay-limestone hill of Pavie, Château Saint-Georges Côte Pavie has the châteaux Pavie and La Gaffelière as immediate neighbours. It also includes a plot situated right next to the Ausone vineyard. Today, the Massons are striving to make the family heritage a perfect reflection of its outstanding terroir for future generations.

CHÂTEAU SOUTARD

AN ESTATE
GATHERED AROUND
A FARM AND
A WATERMILL

With three thousand square meters of roof surface and a classic eighteenth-century architecture, Château Soutard proudly overlooks the valley and plateau of Saint-Émilion, whose high church steeple may be glimpsed nearby. Incomparably noble and elegant, Château Soutard has been synonymous with strength and authority for many centuries. On a turn of the road, a wrought-iron gate opens out onto an alley of lime trees. At the end of it, one may catch a glimpse of the massive mansion with two farm buildings on each side. Le Mayne de Soutard was mentioned as early as 1513 as an estate gathered around a farm and a watermill. Jean Coutures, a Saint-Émilion bourgeois and jurat, bought Soutard in 1699. His daughter Marie increased the surface of the property and built the main aisle of the château, which was completed in 1762. Her son followed in her footsteps, landscaping a garden and building some outhouses. A trained engineer with a passion for vine-growing, he did some thorough work in the vineyard, digging furrows and making Soutard an early pioneer of the technique of row planting, still unknown at the time. Later, the Ligneris family proudly nurtured Soutard's destiny until 2006, when it was bought by La Mondiale insurance company with the ambition of developing this twenty-seven-hectare jewel with the utmost respect for its history and terroir.

CHÂTEAU
TERTRE DAUGAY

❧

SOME PLOTS EVEN HAVE A FEW CENTURY-OLD STOCKS.

Tertre Daugay owes its name to its privileged situation. An observation tower used to stand here in the Middle Ages, informing the Saint-Émilion people of any attack. And the *tertre du guet* — the watchtower hill — like a lookout over a sea of vines, has been watching over the château's reputation for centuries. Long ago, at the watchman's call, the guards would rush to the city to protect it from possible invaders. Since 1978, the château has been the property of Count Léo de Malet Roquefort, also the owner of Château La Gaffelière, a First Great Classified Growth of Saint-Émilion. The Tertre Daugay estate had belonged to his family before, and he had always promised himself to acquire it as soon as he found a chance to do so.

Since buying the château, he has been busy renovating and improving both the vineyard and cellars, keeping as many old vinestocks as he could in order to ensure the quality of the wine. Some plots even have a few century-old stocks, whose roots plunge several meters deep, absorbing the mineral wealth in the soil. The building of a new barrel cellar recently confirmed this search for quality improvement.

CHÂTEAU
VILLEMAURINE

In the seventh century AD, not long before the monk Émilion arrived in the region, the Moors set up a fortified camp in a place that was first called Ville Maure, then Villemaurine, a name most probably inherited from these ancient times. This is also the uncommon name for this vineyard, ideally situated near the northeast walls of the city of Saint-Émilion.

A passionate lover of wine and winemaking, Justin Onclin bought Château Villemaurine in 2007. Driven by a desire to constitute a family heritage and to make his own wines, he was seduced by the estate's potential — seven hectares, in the heart of the Saint-Émilion limestone plateau; the appeal of both a history-laden place and a very promising terroir. The vineyard is run with precise and skilful care that shows evidence of the owner's painstaking philosophy. The new cutting-edge vathouse and barrel cellar are a symbol of this new life, and meeting and reception spaces are also available to help all visitors to enjoy the assets of the property. The huge, one-of-a-kind cellars are enlivened by light and sound animations that include storytelling, historical knowledge and scenography. Today, Villemaurine, yearning to be discovered, proves to be a spiritual and sensorial experience.

VILLEMAURINE
PROVES TO BE
A SPIRITUAL AND
SENSORIAL
EXPERIENCE.

CHÂTEAU
YON FIGEAC

EXTENSIVE WORK
WAS UNDERTAKEN
ON THE LAND
IN ORDER TO BRING
BACK YON FIGEAC
TO ITS FORMER
NOBILITY.

Yon tells the name of the place where the vineyard is located, as is often the case with the names of Saint-Émilion wine châteaux. The same name is found in several other wine properties nearby. Yon Figeac was created in the nineteenth century, when it was probably carved out of the larger Figeac estate. Located on the hill, in the heart of the Saint-Émilion appellation, it was bought in 2005 by Alain Château, a businessman of strong convictions, whose love for the vine and the earth led him to start a new life in winemaking. As soon as he arrived on the property, the investor decided to renovate the vineyard, which grows cabernet franc and merlot. Extensive work was undertaken on the land in order to bring back Yon Figeac to its former nobility. Wine comes first! Soon, the château and other buildings will be renovated in their original nineteenth-century style, quite typical of the region and reminiscent of Cheval Blanc and Laroze, its closest neighbour.

CLOS DE
L'ORATOIRE

Clos de L'Oratoire is a property of the von Neippergs, a famous family of German-born landowners who also own the Châteaux Canon La Gaffelière and La Mondotte in Saint-Émilion. Located on the northeast hill of Saint-Émilion, the estate covers a surface of ten hectares. Its history began in 1969, when a few plots — and all the winemaking that went with them — were separated from the main vineyard of Château Peyreau in order to be classified in their own right at the first revision of the Saint-Émilion classification. The request was accepted and the Clos de L'Oratoire was born. However, it was not until 1991 that Stephan von Neipperg took charge of its full management, gave a new impulse to the winemaking and elevated this grand cru to entirely new heights.

ITS HISTORY BEGAN IN 1969.

CLOS DES
JACOBINS

IN MEDIEVAL TIMES, IT WAS A PROPERTY OF THE DOMINICAN MONASTERY.

Just a few steps away from Saint-Émilion, the Clos des Jacobins, after a long interruption, seems to be born again. In medieval times, it was a property of the Dominican monastery, from which only a wall — called "la Grande Muraille" — remains. In the fourteenth century, the monks deserted it and moved into town. In 2004, the place was purchased by Bernard Decoster, the Limoges-born heir of the Legrand electrical company, and his son Thibaut. They did considerable work on the property, including the château, which shows an entirely renovated face to the visitor.

Thibaut and his wife Magali live at the château with their young children on a permanent basis. Today, they bring out the best of this vineyard — which has been cultivated since the seventeenth century — sharing their passion with their friends and guests in a warm, contemporary atmosphere.

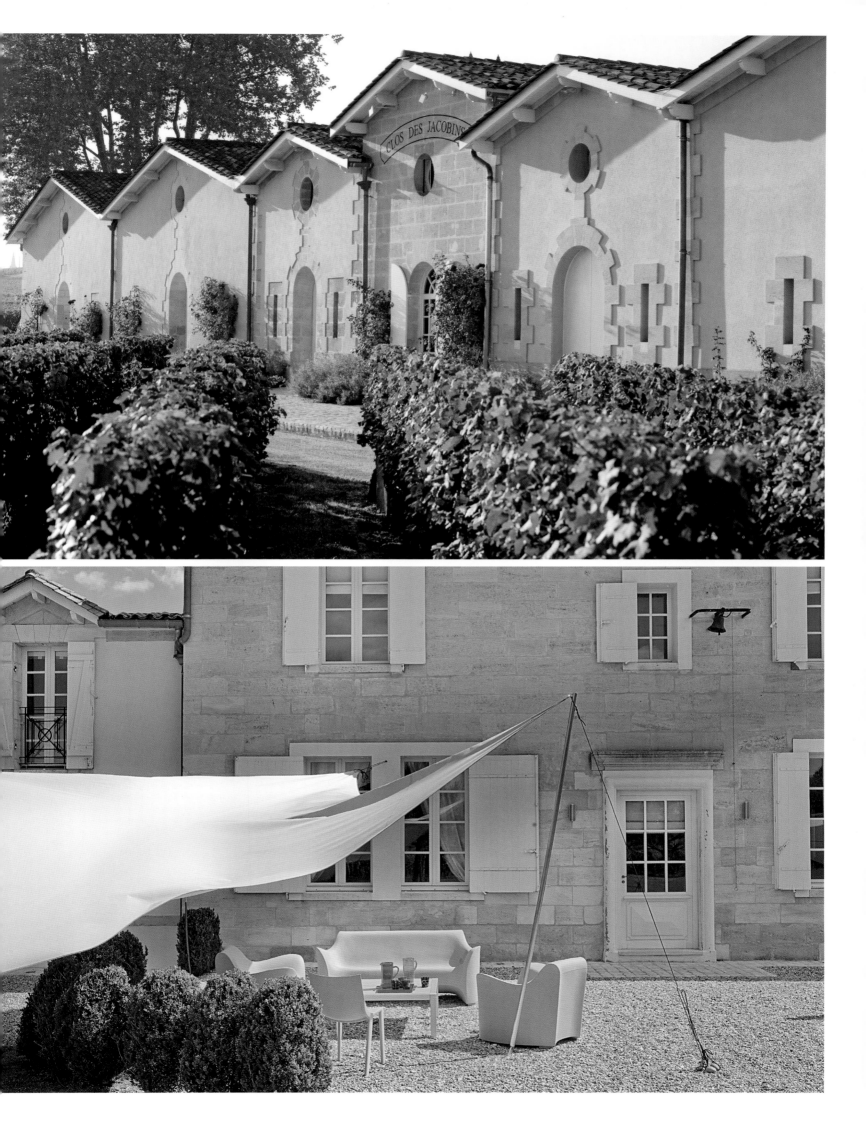

CLOS
SAINT-MARTIN

CHARMING AND REMINISCENT OF A REFINED LIFESTYLE

The former presbytery of the Saint-Martin parish, surrounded by its garden and only one and a third hectares of vineyard, is the smallest in size of all great classified growths in the appellation. Standing on the clay-limestone plateau of Saint-Émilion, facing Bellevue and between the Châteaux Beauséjour and Beau-Séjour Bécot, it enjoys an exceptional location. The Reiffers family, who already owned the nearby Château Les Grandes Murailles, bought the vineyard in 1850. Seen from the courtyard, the house and its huge front door look slightly stern; but seen from the vineyard, the Art Deco pediment, the fountain hiding in the growth of a huge arbutus tree, the seemingly endless terrace and the square-shaped well protected by a glazed tile roof are utterly charming and reminiscent of a refined lifestyle. The cellar is actually a doll cellar — its new oak barrels are lovingly tended by Sophie Fourcade Reiffers, the descendant of a family who settled in Saint-Émilion as early as 1643.

COUVENT
DES JACOBINS

Built in the thirteenth century, the Couvent des Jacobins epitomizes the hazards of history as well as its continuity. Rose-Noëlle Borde, the current descendant of the Joinaud-Borde family, which has owned the estate for 106 years, would have earned the approbation of her grandfather, who was known to say to his children and grandchildren: "I am putting this estate into your hands. If you have any self-respect, you will know it is your duty to leave it in a better shape than when you inherited it." Located in the heart of the medieval city, the place firmly shows its unique character inasmuch that all bottling is done "at the convent", while great care is taken of its architectural treasures and flower gardens left by the Dominican preachers — who, by the way, were also accomplished winemakers. Their wine used to be prized by the Court of England.

Throughout the years, this historical Saint-Émilion land-mark has been renovated stone by stone by the Joinaud-Borde family, who preserved its style with utmost care. The preachers' former bakery was converted into a tasting and reception room that sums up the spirit of this remarkable architectural complex, not to forget the magnificent under-ground stone quarries that run beneath the gardens and buildings and are now used as cellars. At the head of her 10.7 hectares of vineyard, Rose-Noëlle Borde claims to be no more than a temporary caretaker in this jewel of a convent, keeping its memory alive.

FIRST GREAT CLASSIFIED GROWTHS OF SAINT-ÉMILION

CHÂTEAU CHEVAL BLANC
33330 Saint-Émilion
Tél. : +33 (0) 557 555 555
www.chateau-chevalblanc.com
contact@chateau-chevalblanc.com

CHÂTEAU ANGÉLUS
Mazerat – 33330 Saint-Émilion
Tél. : +33 (0) 557 247 139
www.chateau-angelus.com
chateau-angelus@chateau-angelus.com

CHÂTEAU BEAUSÉJOUR
33330 Saint-Émilion
Tél. : +33 (0) 557 247 161
www.beausejourhdl.com
beausejourhdl@beausejourhdl.com

CHÂTEAU BEAU-SÉJOUR BÉCOT
33330 Saint-Émilion
Tél. : +33 (0) 557 744 687
www.beausejour-becot.com
contact@beausejour-becot.com

CHÂTEAU BÉLAIR-MONANGE
Ets Jean-Pierre Moueix
54, quai du Priourat – BP 129
33502 Libourne Cedex
Tél. : +33 (0) 557 517 896
Fax : +33 (0) 557 517 979
www.moueix.com
info@jpmoueix.com

CHÂTEAU CANON
– BP 22 - 33330 Saint-Émilion
Tél. : +33 (0) 557 552 345
Fax : +33 (0) 557 246 800
www.chateau-canon.com
contact@chateau-canon.com

CHÂTEAU DE FIGEAC
33330 Saint-Émilion
Tél. : +33 (0) 557 247 226
www.chateau-figeac.com
chateau-figeac@chateau-figeac.com

CHÂTEAU LA GAFFELIÈRE
33330 Saint-Émilion
Tél. : +33 (0) 557 247 215
www.chateau-la-gaffeliere.com
contact@chateau-la-gaffeliere.com

CHÂTEAU MAGDELAINE
Ets Jean-Pierre Moueix, 54, quai du Priourat
BP 129 – 33502 Libourne Cedex
Tél. : +33 (0) 557 517 896
www.moueix.com
info@jpmoueix.com

CHÂTEAU PAVIE
Domaine de Pavie - 33330 Saint-Émilion
Tél. : +33 (0) 557 554 343
www.vignoblesperse.com
contact@vignoblesperse.com

CHÂTEAU PAVIE MACQUIN
33330 Saint Émilion
Tél. : + 33 (0) 557 247 423
www.pavie-macquin.com
pavie-macquin@nicolas-thienpont.com

CHÂTEAU TROPLONG MONDOT
33330 Saint-Émilion
Tél. : +33 (0) 557 553 205
www.chateau.troplong.mondot.com
contact@chateau-troplong-mondot.com

CHÂTEAU TROTTEVIEILLE
Société Borie-Manoux,
86, cours Balguerie Stuttenberg
33300 Bordeaux
Tél. : +33 (0) 556 000 070
www.borie-manoux.fr
domaines@borie-manoux.fr

CLOS FOURTET
1 Châtelet Sud – 33330 Saint-Émilion
Tél. : +33 (0) 557 247 090
www.closfourtet.com
closfourtet@closfourtet.com

LIST OF THE CHÂTEAUX

LIST OF THE CHÂTEAUX

GREAT CLASSIFIED GROWTHS OF SAINT-ÉMILION

CHÂTEAU BALESTARD LA TONNELLE

Jacques CAPDEMOURLIN

Tél. : +33 5 57 74 62 06

Fax : +33 5 57 74 59 34

www.vignoblescapdemourlin.com

contact@vignoblescapdemourlin.com

CHÂTEAU BELLEFONT-BELCIER

Jacques BERREBI, Dominique HEBRARD, Alain LAGUILLAUMIE

Tél. : +33 5 57 24 72 16

Fax : +33 5 57 74 45 06

www.bellefont-belcier.com

chateau.bellefont-belcier@wanadoo.fr

CHÂTEAU BELLEVUE

Hubert de BOÜARD de LAFOREST

Tél. : +33 5 57 24 71 39

Fax :+33 5 57 24 68 56

www.chateau-angelus.com

chateau-angelus@chateau-angelus.com

CHÂTEAU BERGAT

Philippe CASTEJA

Tél. : +33 5 56 00 00 70

Fax : +33 5 57 87 48 61

domaines@borie-manoux.fr

CHÂTEAU BERLIQUET

Vicomte Patrick de LESQUEN

Tél. : +33 5 57 24 70 48

www.chateau-berliquet.com

chateau.berliquet@wanadoo.fr

CHÂTEAU CADET BON

Guy and Michèle RICHARD

Tél. : +33 5 57 74 43 20

www.cadet-bon.com

chateau.cadet.bon@terre-net.fr

CHÂTEAU CADET-PIOLA

Claire THOMAS-CHENARD

Tél. : +33 5 57 24 71 41

Fax : +33 5 57 74 42 80

www.chateau-larmande.com

contact@soutard-larmande.com

CHÂTEAU CANON LA GAFFELIÈRE

Comte Stephan VON NEIPPERG

Tél. : +33 5 57 24 71 33

Fax : +33 5 57 24 67 95

www.neipperg.com

info@neipperg.com

CHÂTEAU CAP DE MOURLIN

Jacques CAPDEMOURLIN

Tél. : +33 5 57 74 62 06

Fax : +33 5 57 74 59 34

www.vignoblescapdemourlin.com

contact@vignoblescapdemourlin.com

CHÂTEAU CHAUVIN

Béatrice ONDET and Marie-France FEVRIER

Tél. : +33 5 57 24 76 25

Fax : +33 5 57 74 41 34

www.chateauchauvin.com

chateauchauvingcc@wanadoo.fr

CHÂTEAU CORBIN

Sébastien and Anabelle BARDINET

Tél. : +33 5 57 25 20 30

Fax : +33 5 57 25 22 20

www.chateau-corbin.com

contact@chateau-corbin.com

CHÂTEAU CORBIN MICHOTTE

Emmanuel BOIDRON

Tél. : +33 5 57 51 64 88

Fax : +33 5 57 51 56 30

vignoblesjnboidron@wanadoo.fr

CHÂTEAU DASSAULT

Laurence BRUN

Tél. : +33 5 57 55 10 00

Fax : +33 5 57 55 10 01

www.chateaudassault.com

lbv@chateaudassault.com

CHÂTEAU DESTIEUX

Christian DAURIAC

Tél. : +33 5 57 24 77 44

Fax : +33 5 57 40 37 42

www.vignobles-dauriac.com

contact@vignobles-dauriac.com

CHÂTEAU FAURIE DE SOUCHARD

Geoffroy and Thibaut SCIARD

Tél. : +335 57 74 03 80

Fax : 05 57 74 43 96

www.fauriedesouchard.com

fauriedesouchard@wanadoo.fr

CHÂTEAU FLEUR CARDINALE

Dominique and Florence DECOSTER

Tél. : +33 5 57 40 14 05

Fax : +33 5 57 40 28 62

www.chateau-fleurcardinale.com

fleurcardinale@wanadoo.fr

CHÂTEAU FONPLÉGADE

Olivier NOUET

Tél. : +33 5 57 74 43 11

Fax : +33 5 57 74 44 67

www.adamsfrenchvineyards.fr

karine.queron@fonplegade.fr

CHÂTEAU FONROQUE

Alain MOUEIX

Tél. : +33 5 57 24 60 02

Fax : +33 5 57 24 74 59

www.chateaufonroque.com

info@chateaufonroque.com

CHÂTEAU FRANC MAYNE

Griet and Hervé LAVIALE

Tél. : +33 5 57 24 62 61

Fax : +33 5 57 24 68 25

www.chateaufrancmayne.com

info@chateaufrancmayne.com

CHÂTEAU GRAND CORBIN

Philippe GIRAUD

Tél. : +33 5 57 24 70 62

Fax : +33 5 57 74 47 18

www.grand-corbin.com

contact@grand-corbin.com

CHÂTEAU GRAND CORBIN-DESPAGNE

François DESPAGNE

Tél. : +33 5 57 51 08 38

Fax : +33 5 57 51 29 18

www.grand-corbin-despagne.com

f-despagne@grand-corbin-despagne.com

CHÂTEAU GRAND MAYNE

Famille NONY

Tél. : +33 5 57 74 42 50

www.grand-mayne.com

grand-mayne@grand-mayne.com

CHÂTEAU GRAND PONTET

Sylvie POURQUET-BÉCOT

Tél. : +33 557 74 46 88

Fax : +33 5 57 74 45 31

chateau.grand-pontet@wanadoo.fr

CHÂTEAU GUADET

Guy PETRUS-LIGNAC

Tél. : + 33 5 57 74 40 04

Fax : + 33 5 57 24 63 50

www.guadet.com

chateauguadet@orange.fr

CHÂTEAU HAUT-CORBIN

Philippe DAMBRINE

Tél. : +33 5 57 97 02 82

Fax : +33 5 57 97 02 84

www.hautcorbin.com

cantemerle@cantemerle.fr

CHÂTEAU HAUT-SARPE

Jean-François JANOUEIX

Tél. : +33 5 57 51 41 86

Fax : +33 5 57 51 53 16

www.josephjanoueix.com

info@j-janoueix-bordeaux.com

CHÂTEAU L'ARROSÉE

Jean-philippe CAILLE

Tél. : +33 5 57 24 98 84

Fax : +33 5 57 24 66 46

www.chateaularrosee.com

contact@chateaularrosee.com

CHÂTEAU LA CLOTTE

Nelly MOULIERAC

Tél. : +33 5 57 24 66 85

Fax : +33 5 57 24 79 67

www.chateaulaclotte.com

contact@chateaulaclotte.com

CHÂTEAU LA COUSPAUDE

Jean-claude AUBERT

Tél. : +33 5 57 40 15 76

Fax : +33 5 57 40 10 14

www.la-couspaude.com

info@la-couspaude.com

CHÂTEAU LA DOMINIQUE

Yannick EVENOU

Tél. : +33 5 57 51 31 36

Fax : +33 5 57 51 63 04

www.vignobles.fayat.com

contact@vignobles.fayat.com

CHÂTEAU LA MARZELLE

Jacqueline SCION

Tél. : +33 5 57 55 10 65

www.chateaulamarzelle.com

chateau@lamarzelle.com

CHÂTEAU LA SERRE

Luc D'ARFEUILLE

Tél. : +33 5 57 24 71 38

Fax : +33 5 57 24 63 01

darfeuille.luc@wanadoo.fr

CHÂTEAU LA TOUR DU PIN

LVMH, groupe Albert FRÈRE

Tél. : +33 5 57 55 55 55

Fax : 05 57 55 55 50

c.favre@chateau-chevalblanc.com

CHÂTEAU LA TOUR DU PIN FIGEAC

Famille Giraud BELIVIER

Tél. : +33 5 57 51 06 10

www.vins-giraud-belivier.com

giraud.belivier@wanadoo.fr

CHÂTEAU LA TOUR FIGEAC

Otto RETTENMAIER

Tél. : +33 5 57 51 77 62

Fax : +33 5 57 25 36 92

www.latourfigeac.com

info@latourfigeac.com

CHÂTEAU LANIOTE

Arnaud and Florence de la FILOLIE

Tél. : +33 5 57 24 70 80

Fax : +33 5 57 24 60 11

www.laniote.com

contact@laniote.com

CHÂTEAU LARCIS DUCASSE

Nicolas THIENPONT

Tél. : +33 5 57 24 70 84

Fax : +33 5 57 24 64 00

www.larcis-ducasse.com

contact@larcis-ducasse.com

CHÂTEAU LARMANDE

Claire THOMAS-CHENARD

Tél. : +33 5 57 24 71 41

Fax : +33 5 57 74 42 80

www.chateau-larmande.com

contact@soutard-larmande.com

CHÂTEAU LAROQUE

Xavier BEAUMARTIN

Tél. : +33 5 57 24 77 28

Fax : +33 5 57 24 63 65

www.chateau-laroque.com

contact@chateau-laroque.com

CHÂTEAU LAROZE

Guy MESLIN

Tél. : +33 5 57 24 79 79

Fax : +33 5 57 24 79 80

www.laroze.com

info@laroze.com

CHÂTEAU LE PRIEURÉ

Aline and Paul GOLDSCHMIDT

Tél. : +33 5 57 51 64 58

Fax : +33 5 57 51 41 56

www.baronneguichard.com

Info@baronneguichard.com

CHÂTEAU LES GRANDES MURAILLES

Sophie FOURCADE

Tél. : +33 5 57 24 71 09

Fax : +33 5 57 24 69 72

www.lesgrandesmurailles.fr

lesgrandesmurailles@wanadoo.Fr

CHÂTEAU MATRAS

Véronique GABORIAUD-BERNARD

Tél. : +33 5 57 51 52 39

Fax : +33 5 57 51 70 19

www.vignoblesgaboriaud.com

contact@vignoblesgaboriaud.com

CHÂTEAU MONBOUSQUET
Gérard and Chantal PERSE
Tél. : +33 5 57 55 43 43
www.vignoblesperse.com
contact@vignoblesperse.com

CHÂTEAU MOULIN DU CADET
Pierre BLOIS
Tél. : +33 5 57 55 00 50
Fax : +33 5 57 51 63 44
moulinducadet@wanadoo.fr

CHÂTEAU PAVIE DECESSE
Gérard and Chantal PERSE
Tél. : +33 5 57 55 43 43
www.vignoblesperse.com
contact@vignoblesperse.com

CHÂTEAU PETIT FAURIE DE SOUTARD
Jacques CAPDEMOURLIN
Tél. : +33 5 57 74 62 06
Fax : +33 5 57 74 59 34
www.vignoblescapdemourlin.com
contact@vignoblescapdemourlin.com

CHÂTEAU RIPEAU
Famille de WILDE
Tél. : +33 5 57 74 41 41
Fax : +33 5 57 74 41 57
www.chateauripeau.com
chateau.ripeau@wanadoo.fr

CHÂTEAU SAINT-GEORGES CÔTE PAVIE
Famille MASSON
Tél. : +33 5 57 74 44 23
Fax : + 33 2 40 47 97 13
marcadejerome@orange.fr

CHÂTEAU SOUTARD
Claire THOMAS-CHENARD
Tél. : +33 5 57 24 71 41
Fax : +33 5 57 74 42 80
www.chateausoutard.com
contact@soutard-larmande.com

CHÂTEAU TERTRE DAUGAY
Comte Léo de MALET ROQUEFORT
Tel +33 5 57 56 40 80
www.chateau-tertre-dauguay.com
contact@chateau-tertre-dauguay.com

CHÂTEAU VILLEMAURINE
Justin ONCLIN
Tél. : +33 5 57 74 47 30
Fax : +33 5 57 24 63 09
www.villemaurine.com
contact@villemaurine.com

CHÂTEAU YON FIGEAC
Alain CHATEAU
Tél. : +33 2 41 78 33 66
Fax : +33 2 41 78 68 47
www.vignobles-alainchateau.com
info@vignobles-alainchateau.com

CLOS DE L'ORATOIRE
Comte Stephan VON NEIPPERG
Tél. : +33 5 57 24 71 33
Fax : +33 5 57 24 67 95
www.neipperg.com
info@neipperg.com

CLOS DES JACOBINS
Bernard and Thibaut DECOSTER
Tél. : +33 5 57 24 70 14
Fax : +33 5 57 24 68 08
www.closdesjacobins.com
couventdesjacobins@dbmail.com

CLOS SAINT-MARTIN
Sophie FOURCADE
Tél. : +33 5 57 24 71 09
Fax : +33 5 57 24 69 72
www.lesgrandesmurailles.fr
lesgrandesmurailles@wanadoo.fr

COUVENT DES JACOBINS
Rose-Nöelle BORDE
Tél. : +33 5 57 24 70 66
Fax : +33 5 57 24 62 51
www.couventdesjacobins.fr
dpomarede@club-internet.fr

ACKNOWLEDGMENTS

The Groupement de Premiers Grands Crus Classés de Saint-Émilion
and the Association de Grands Crus Classés de Saint-Émilion would like to thank Serena Sutcliffe,
Thierry Manoncourt and François Querre.
Guillaume de Laubier, Emmanuelle Ponsan-Dantin and Béatrice Massenet have special thanks for
Hubert de Boüard, president of Groupement de Premiers Grands Crus Classés of Saint-Émilion,
and Alain Moueix, president of the Association de Grands Crus Classés of Saint-Émilion.

All photographs by Guillaume de Laubier except on pages:
75, top: © Hervé Lefebvre/Twin
163, bottom: © Château Grand Corbin-Despagne
164, bottom: © Château Grand Mayne

Graphic design: Laurence Maillet
Editorial coordination: Nathalie Chapuis
Translated from French by Sophie Brissaud

Cataloging-in-Publication Data has been applied for and may be obtained from the Library of Congress.

ISBN: 978-1-58479-944-3

© 2011 Éditions de La Martinière — Ateliers Saveurs,
an imprint of La Martinière Groupe, Paris

Originally published in French under the title *Esprit des vins: Crus classés de Saint-Émilion* by Éditions de La Martinière — Ateliers Saveurs, an imprint of La Martinière Groupe, Paris

Printed and bound in Hong Kong, China
10 9 8 7 6 5 4 3 2 1

Abrams books are available at special discounts when purchased in quantity for premiums and promotions as well as fundraising or educational use. Special editions can also be created to specification. For details, contact specialsales@abramsbooks.com or the address below.

115 West 18th Street
New York, NY 10011
www.abramsbooks.com